WHAT'S GOING WELL?

WHAT'S GOING WELL?

The Question That Changes Everything

GREG BELL

THREE STAR PUBLISHING
PORTLAND, OREGON

Three Star Publishing
7327 SW Barnes Road #524
Portland, OR 97225
Tel: (503) 963-8817

Ordering information
Special discounts are available on quantity purchases. For details, visit: gregbellspeaks.com/books

Printed in the United States of America

Copyediting by Michelle Polizzi
Book cover design by Catherine Veraghen of happy, inc.; gethappyinc.com
Interior design by Jennifer Omner of ALL Publications; allpublications.com

ISBN: 978-1-935313-00-7

First Edition

This book is dedicated to both the
optimists and the pessimists around the world.

contents

introduction

"For there is nothing good or bad,
but thinking that makes it so."
~ Shakespeare, Hamlet

Since I can remember, I have been preoccupied with the question of why some people reach their full potential and others don't. This obsession led me to quit the practice of law and start a seminar company where I am fortunate enough to provide inspirational keynotes and seminars to some of the most interesting and noteworthy organizations in the world.

My first book, *Water The Bamboo: Unleashing The Potential Of Teams And Individuals*, describes a philosophy and strategy that connects back to the biology of Giant Timber Bamboo. This amazing plant takes up to five years before it sprouts, but once it enters this phase, it grows 90 feet in 60 days. In the book, I encourage individuals and teams to nurture their dreams with patience, persistence, and self-discipline. You have to keep watering the bamboo, even when it does not seem like it's growing and feels like it never will. Knowing the big picture helps us stay focused and persistent, long before results come. Over the years, I have heard from many people, near and far, about how much the book and philosophy has helped them achieve remarkable results, so I understand the value of getting these lessons down on paper to share with people. I am thrilled that the book continues to help people reach their goals.

I decided to put pen to paper again for this book, because lately I've noticed a recurring pattern of negativity that's troubling and unproductive, and I wanted to provide an antidote. When individuals and organizations focus on what's going wrong, even those deemed successful by most measures, it has a *dramatic*—and *traumatic*—negative impact on everything from personal health and well-being, to relationships with friends and family, to productivity and work quality.

The *What's Going Well* mindset, on the other hand, is a habit and practice of positivity that builds more optimism and success the more it's used. This is an upward spiral. The principles outlined in this book, when applied in a thoughtful and systematic way, will help correct the common imbalance towards negativity and provide better outcomes for business, education and health.

Positive Psychology is backed up by mounds of research and data that offers a clear rebuttal to naysaying. Individuals and organizations that embrace the *What's Going Well* mindset will realize significant benefits in the form of:

- increased productivity;
- better relationships;
- greater contentment;
- better health;
- improved employee and client retention;
- more clarity about what is important; and
- higher levels of employee engagement.

How to Use This Book

There are a few ways to use this book. It is meant to be an interactive, customizable tool that helps you practically incorporate the *What's Going Well* mindset into your life. I've demystified the principles to make them actionable and easy to understand. Some people will find it useful to work alone, where others may find it helpful to create a *What's Going Well* reading club.

In addition to reading the book, I encourage you to journal your *What's Going Well* journey. You can use the *What's Going Well? 90-Day Companion Journal* I have designed, or any journal of your choosing. The important thing is that you journal. **Throughout the book this icon ☼ will denote journal exercises.** The 90-day companion journal contains inspirational quotes, space for you to write about *What's Going Well* daily, and blank note pages in the back for your reflections on the journal exercises. I urge you to make a commitment to journal 10 to 15 minutes daily for 90 days—this small investment will yield surprising results. The *What's Going Well? 90-Day Companion Journal* is designed to help you keep track of the benefits of the *What's Going Well* mindset. You will want a journal solely for *What's Going Well* so that you have a place to refer back to that's dedicated to the positives in your life.

Subscribe to the *What's Going Well* journey emails
Go to gregbellspeaks.com/wgw to subscribe to the *What's Going Well* journey emails, a companion to the *What's Going Well* book and journal. And don't forget to get a copy of the *What's Going Well? 90-Day Companion Journal*: gregbellspeaks. com/books

Each chapter of this book builds upon the next to support you as you embrace the *What's Going Well* mindset. The chapters introduce the underlying principles and provide tools you can use in daily life. Here's what's included:

Chapter 1: The Power of *What's Going Well*—the life-altering benefits of living a life that embraces *What's Going Well*.

Chapter 2: How the *What's Going Well* Mindset Works—the science behind *What's Going Well* and how it affects the brain.

Chapter 3: Understanding Our What's Going Wrong Default—insight into our dominant mindset and its impact on our lives.

Chapter 4: Making *What's Going Well* a Habit—creating the shift from what's going wrong to *What's Going Well*.

Chapter 5: Applying *What's Going Well* Personally—how to apply the *What's Going Well* mindset to your personal life and relationships.

Chapter 6: Applying *What's Going Well* Professionally—how to apply the *What's Going Well* mindset to your professional life.

Chapter 7: What About When "Nothing" is Going Well?—the benefit of *What's Going Well* when things are going poorly.

Chapter 8: Final Thoughts—a recap and send-off.

I believe that *What's Going Well* is one of the most effective tools for helping an individual or a group reach their highest potential and experience well-being. It is my hope that by the time you finish reading this book, you will feel as strongly about the value of embracing a *What's Going Well* mindset as I do. I also hope reading this book will be enjoyable and give you useful tools and insights to change your life for the better; however, developing a *What's Going Well* mindset takes focus and discipline. I hope you're up for the challenge.

one

The Power of *What's Going Well*

"People are disturbed not by things,
but by the view they take of them."
~ Epictetus

We all have had moments where friends thank us for surprising reasons. The one I want to tell you about happened over the phone years ago one spring. For me, it brought into focus a way of thinking I'd taken for granted and put me on the journey that led me to write this book. During a phone call, a friend referenced a moment that I barely remembered, but what had seemed insignificant to me had clearly meant a lot to him. What I did remember is that I'd seen him in a coffee shop a week prior to the call, and my normally upbeat friend looked miserable on that particular morning. His customary big smile was replaced by a somber look and he was obviously frustrated about something. I'd cautiously made my way to sit at his table and tried to cheer him up. He reminded me of this conversation and then said: "Thank you for asking me *What's going well?* the other day. It really helped me get out of my bad mood and got me to think and reflect on all the good in my life."

It seemed like such a small moment, but I remembered it once he brought it back to mind for me. He'd been thrown off a bit by the question and after thinking for a while he said that he and his wife were getting along a lot better, he mentioned he was looking forward to a long run by the river later that afternoon, he said that his kids were doing pretty well in school, he said he had just landed a new client, and more. This went on for about 30 minutes until I had to leave for a meeting. As I made it to the door of the coffee shop, he had seemed more at ease.

I hung up the phone that day feeling grateful that I had helped a friend, but the part that struck me was that, while I vaguely remembered asking him *What's going well?*, I had never asked the same into the mirror. The call motivated me to try on *What's going well?* for myself. Like my friend, I went on my own *What's going well?* journey. Prior to immersing myself in *What's going well?*, I had a pretty good life, but like many people I spent a lot of my time focusing on problems and what was going wrong. I wasn't ungrateful, I just did not pay focused attention to all the good in my life. My days started exhausted from a bad night's sleep, waking to a blaring alarm. Immediately the "negaholic" in my head would start chattering nonstop about random worries and concerns, saying things like, "At my age I should be further ahead;" "What if there is an accident and I am late to work;" "What if they missed something at my last physical checkup;" "Will I have enough money to retire," etc. To add to the stress, I'd tune into the news. Like many, this was my "normal." The pattern changed once I committed to focusing on *What's going well?* and made it a habit. Things shifted dramatically, I became happier and experienced greater well-being. In a short time, I came to realize that a positive life is not something that just happens to us—it is something we create by focusing on and savoring *What's going well?* around us. Not only did I apply this concept personally but also I began a 15-year journey, researching and incorporating the *What's Going Well* mindset, principles and concepts into my work with leaders and teams. I found that the *What's Going Well* mindset is rooted in real science, has real benefits, and like any skill, can be learned and cultivated. By engaging in this work, I have had the privilege of witnessing the power for positive change that resides within each of us. Since the day my friend called, I have had a burning desire to share the *What's Going Well* mindset, ideas and practices far and wide.

> *"We don't see things as they are,*
> *we see them as we are."*
> *~ Anais Nin*

A *What's Going Well* Mindset Helps Us Find the Wind at Our Backs

Imagine riding a bicycle against a strong headwind. You notice that the headwind slows your progress as you pedal. Now, imagine turning your bike around and riding with the wind at your back, helping you progress faster and pedal easier. Initially, you'll notice it is much easier to pedal with the tailwind than against the headwind, but soon you won't notice the tailwind at all—even though it is still there.[1] It's an interesting phenomenon that carries over to our daily lives.

Our tendency to forget the tailwind shows up in many ways. For example, when we get involved in a new relationship or obtain a new possession, we typically will be very appreciative and give it our full attention at first. After the initial excitement, the newness wears off and we get accustomed to people and things and we take them for granted. When this happens, we stop treating them as special and we pay less attention to them. Psychologists call this *hedonic habituation*.[2] That's why it is sometimes easier to express gratitude to a total stranger than someone you see every day. *Hedonic habituation* is also what causes a visitor to our hometown to enjoy and appreciate things that we pay little attention to. It causes us to ignore *What's Going Well* and begin to believe that the grass is greener on the other side of the fence. Becoming accustomed to what's familiar, we start looking for something new or better instead of appreciating what we already have. In reality, the grass is greener where we water it. Appreciation makes most anything thrive.

> *"You don't know what you've got 'til it's gone."*
> *~ Joni Mitchell*

---

1   Davidai, S., & Gilovich, T. (2016). The headwinds/tailwinds asymmetry: An availability bias in assessments of barriers and blessings. *Journal of Personality and Social Psychology, 111(6)*, 835–851.

2   Brickman, P., & Campbell, D. T. (1971). Hedonic relativism and planning the good society. In M. H. Appley (Ed.), *Adaptation-level theory* (pp. 287–302). New York, NY: Academic Press.

Too often, we appreciate things more when they are threatened or go away entirely. We don't appreciate our good health until we are sick or injured. We don't appreciate a good manager until we experience a bad one. We don't appreciate a loved one until we lose them. The *What's Going Well* mindset helps highlight the people, things, and experiences we may be taking for granted. It reminds us to appreciate the wind at our backs.

> *"Tell me what you pay attention to and*
> *I will show you who you are."*
> *~ Jose Oretega Gasset*

The magic of the *What's Going Well* mindset is that it gets us to proactively notice the wind that is already there. Wherever we are, there's always something going well. And if we're in the habit of noticing the wind at our backs, we'll always find it. Here are some examples of small things to be grateful for: Our kid gives us a hug for no reason, the clerk offers us a coupon for a few dollars off, our car starts in the bitter cold, the back pain isn't so bad today, an old friend reconnects, we find a great book at the library, we catch our connecting flight, our boss gives us the afternoon off, someone holds the door for us, our friends remember our birthday, a stranger smiles at us, someone lets us merge in traffic, our neighbor offers tickets to the game, a majestic old tree provides beauty and shade. No doubt you can relate to many of these examples. If we focus on *What's Going Well* in our lives, we soon discover a bounty of experiences that reveal that there's a lot to be grateful for.

The *What's Going Well* mindset cultivates the skill and concentration to *discover* the things that are going well right where we are. This mindset, which exists at the convergence of philosophy, positive psychology, and neuroscience, suggests that what we pay attention to determines our life experience. When we pay attention to the good things in our lives, we experience better results than when we allow ourselves to focus on faults and imperfections. By focusing on *What's Going Well,* we direct our emotions, thoughts, and behaviors toward the positive, literally creating a better world by choosing where to focus our thoughts.

> *"The aim of Positive Psychology is to catalyze a change in psychology from a preoccupation only with repairing the worst things in life to also building the best qualities in life."*
> ~ Dr. Martin Seligman

What's Going Well Mindset Brings Forth the Positive

The *What's Going Well* mindset has roots in positive psychology. Pioneered by psychologist Dr. Martin Seligman, positive psychology challenges the "disease model" of traditional psychology that focuses on problems of the past. Focusing on what went wrong is a bit like continually picking at a wound and then wondering why it won't heal; instead, positive psychology focuses on looking forward and moving on. Positive psychologists have shown that when patients pay attention to the good in their lives, they feel less depressed and experience greater well-being.[3] This mindset is at the core of strength-based, asset-based, and appreciative approaches found in fields such as education, community development, and

---

3   Seligman, M. E. P. (2011). *Flourish: a visionary new understanding of happiness and well-being.* New York, NY: Free Press.

organizational development. When we focus on the positive, our mood shifts and the world becomes a place of infinite possibilities. Adopting a *What's Going Well* mindset stimulates creativity, expands our thinking, and enhances our sense of well-being.

Positive psychology is nothing new, but the *What's Going Well* mindset provides a tactical approach to integrating it into our lives. Along the way, we'll unpack why it matters so much. By taking a simple and straightforward approach to the *What's Going Well* mindset, positive psychology can become part of how we live.

"If you can't explain it simply, you don't understand it well enough."
~ Albert Einstein

What takes up space in the valuable real estate of our mind is a strong predictor of our happiness and well-being. Without question, it is helpful to talk and think about problems from time to time, because it allows us to understand issues, get support, and devise a plan of action. This is not about blind optimism where you shut out any and all suffering—we can't be blind to our challenges. However, merely pointing out what's going wrong and obsessing over it can often make things much worse than they really are, causing unnecessary worry and frustration. A *What's Going Well* mindset allows us to steer ourselves to a healthier, happier reality.

What's Going Well helps us find the positive aspects in every situation. A *What's Going Well* mindset won't improve the weather, make our favorite sports team win the championship or make our candidate win the election. But it will empower us to *bring our own sunshine* no matter how the weather turns out, how our team plays in the game, or who wins office.

"What we see depends mainly on what we look for."
~ John Lubbock

Please Note:
Although the *What's Going Well* mindset is a complement to psychology and psychiatry, it is not a replacement for getting professional help.

"Appreciate what you have before it turns into what you had."
~ Anonymous

What's Going Well Mindset Leads to Gratitude

Being told to be grateful can be counterproductive because it carries an assumption that we are not grateful—which can make us feel defensive and conjure up feelings of shame and guilt. Part of the simple beauty of asking *"What's Going Well?"* is that we are prompting our minds to focus on the good.

"Your mind will answer most questions if
you learn to relax and wait for the answer."
~ William S. Burroughs

At this point in the book, you may be thinking this is just another positive thinking book and one more person who thinks they have the answer. I don't have the answer. I have the question. Your mind already has the answer and it has many of them. The more you ask *What's Going Well* and develop a *What's Going Well* mindset, the more the brain will sync up the narrative and build a positive story. Thinking about *What's Going Well* allows us to access gratitude on our own terms.

> *"Simplicity is the ultimate sophistication."*
> *~ Leonardo da Vinci*

What's Going Well Feeds the Good Wolf

When we consider how much negativity is around us, it's clear that the forces of what's going wrong are putting in an all-out effort. In order to win the battle of our well-being, it seems we must work twice as hard to develop and maintain a *What's Going Well* mindset. Here is a legend that illustrates the importance of feeding your *What's Going Well* mindset:

A young warrior went to the tribal leader to ask: "What is the secret to life?" The leader responded that a person faces many battles, but the fiercest battle happens in a person's mind between two wolves—a good wolf and a bad wolf, with the two wolves fighting throughout the person's life. The bad wolf says things like "I am a loser. I am a nobody. Things never work out for me." The good wolf says: "I am doing well. Things are bound to work out. I am a success." The thoughts of the bad wolf and the good wolf will do whatever they can to survive inside of us, so that when a small piece of evidence shows itself, we say: "I knew it," and we continually look for more evidence. Confused, the young warrior asked which wolf wins the fight. The tribal leader replied: "The one you are feeding, so feed the right wolf!"

"It is not reality that shapes us, but the lens in which we view reality."
~ *Shawn Achor, Author of* The Happiness Advantage

 journal exercise

What's Going Well Mindset Day

Try *What's Going Well* on for yourself. Pick an ordinary day—a day with nothing special planned—and make it a *What's Going Well* mindset day. Spend the entire day looking only for *What's Going Well* and vow to refrain from complaining or participating in negative conversations. In addition, go media-free for an entire 24-hour period (it's harder than you think). At the end of the day, journal and reflect on the following:

- How do you feel?
- What did you notice?
- What surprised you?

Subscribe to the *What's Going Well* journey emails
at gregbellspeaks.com/wgw

What's Going Well Mindset is Attractive

Deepak Chopra said: "All relationships are a reflection of your relationship with yourself." When you consistently reflect on *What's Going Well*, you can't help but radiate positivity into the world. It starts to become a part of everything you do, and it shows. One leader told me after focusing on the *What's Going Well* mindset for a few months, he not only improved his relationships at work, but the mindset shift especially helped him at home. He said: "The people in my life have noticed the positive change and they come around more." The side benefit of *What's Going Well* is that, very simply, it makes you more likable, and that's another thing going well. (See how it builds?)

Would you like to spend time with someone who is constantly complaining about life, their job, gossiping about friends and coworkers, or putting themselves and others down? Or would you rather spend time with someone who is upbeat despite the challenges they face? The answer is obvious because we are drawn to people with positive attitudes and outlooks. It's up to you to choose who you want to be—adopting a *What's Going Well* mindset will help you gain a positive perspective and attitude, and what you're doing inward will reflect outward. This will make you more likeable and people will want to be a part of your positivity. Of course, problems will still exist and you will need to confide in and rely on some people when challenges arise. This is about establishing a habit and pattern that will have a positive impact on your life.

What's Going Well Reveals the Beauty in Our Lives

"I freed the statue from the stone."
~ Michelangelo

Michelangelo claimed that his main talent was chipping away excess marble to expose the statue. Similarly, a *What's Going Well* mindset reveals and exposes all the good in our lives.

What's Going Well Mindset Shifts Perspective

"Knowledge is having the right answer,
intelligence is having the right question."
~ Unknown

Not only do I start my day with *What's Going Well*, I also begin all my keynote speeches and leadership seminars with a simple, yet powerful, *What's Going Well* exercise. I encourage participants to share things that are going well in their personal and professional lives, and I'm often amazed by what people say after the experience. Energized from the *What's Going Well* interactions and conversations, leaders and executives almost always say, "This was an incredible experience for my team. Why don't we do this more often?" I continually hear from clients that they want to incorporate the *What's Going Well* mindset into their work culture. They, like me, realize the *What's Going Well* mindset is like the secret sauce to engagement, success, and well-being.

Implement *What's Going Well* in Your Organization
Download the FREE *What's Going Well for Teams Guide—a 10 Step Guide to Incorporate What's Going Well in your Organization* at gregbellspeaks.com/wgw-leaders-guide .

The power of the *What's Going Well* mindset is found in the perspective shift it brings. A focus on *What's Going Well* helps us see the world from a positive vantage point, changing our perspective from what we *lack* to what we *have*, from what's *challenging* to what we've *accomplished*, from feeling *burdened and defeated* to feeling *rejuvenated and recharged*. More than a feel-good attitude, it is a mindset that improves our health, relationships, and overall well-being.

If it's all so simple and easy, why doesn't everyone do it? Why aren't you doing it already? Well, life is busy and complicated and we're often tasked with solving problems, so we mostly focus on problems and get in the habit of doing that. Also, asking *"What's Going Well?"* can seem like a little thing, so it becomes easy to ignore, but small things going well add up and make a big difference in your level of happiness, well-being and contentment.

"It's the little details that are vital.
Little things make big things happen."
~ John Wooden

two

How the
What's Going Well Mindset Works

"The fish is the last to know about water."
~ Albert Einstein

Like the fish Einstein references in the quote above, we are often the last to recognize things going well in our lives—unless we intentionally focus on doing just that. Many people are *swimming* in things going well, but they're too caught up in the net of what's going wrong to notice them. Again, we may be doing this as a part of problem-solving and a natural survival instinct, but I'm encouraging you to fight this tendency. We must rule our own brain, instead of allowing it to drag us into unnecessary negativity and discontent.

We all know someone who seems to be 'winning' at life but fails to recognize it. They don't take the time to acknowledge and express gratitude about how good things are and, as a result, remain unhappy and unfulfilled. Watching them, we're reminded that a ful-filled life has less to do with material success or what happens to us and more to do with the *attitude we have* about what happens—our state of mind. If we don't deliberately place our attention on *What's Going Well*, we often default to a focus on the negatives. Intention-ally attending to *What's Going Well* constructs our thoughts and beliefs to foster empathy and compassion for ourselves and others. A *What's Going Well* mindset helps us acknowledge and attend to the good in our lives. Doing so cultivates our sense of well-being and strengthens our capacity to deal with the challenges we face.

We've Been Wired for Negativity

In any given moment, we're bombarded with massive amounts of information. Our brains are constantly filtering what gets our attention because we only have the capacity to focus on a fraction of what we encounter. In this filtering process, our brains are easily dis-tracted because we are wired to pay attention to any new stimulus, especially if we perceive it to be a threat to our survival. This filter-ing causes us to have what psychologists call a *negativity bias*.[4] This was a useful adaptation for our ancestors who might not survive to see another day if they ignored the rustling in the bush. However, an outgrowth of our natural tendency to be hyperaware of danger is that we tend to overlook the good in our lives. Media and society take advantage of this *negativity bias*, feeding us images and stories designed to grab our attention but not necessarily for our benefit.

---

4   Baumeister, R., Bratslavsky, E., Finkenauer, C., & Vohs, D. K. (2001). Bad is stronger than good. *Review of General Pyschology 5*, 323–370.

When our world-view gets shaped by an over consumption of news and social media, we can get an imbalanced perspective believing that we are getting the right ratio of positive and negative. Natural disasters, acts of violence and suicide carry the day in our daily newsfeeds which can overwhelm us with fear and angst. It appears to be getting worse every year.

Thousands of Airplanes Landed Safely at Airports Around the World Today

Imagine the above statement was a headline in the news. Even though it happens every day we would never see this in a headline. The main goal of "the news" is to get our attention, and negativity gets our attention—especially if it is bloody and graphic. Thus, the saying in the news business: "If it bleeds it leads."

Our Fight or Flight System is on Overdrive

The evolutionary benefit of *negativity bias* explains why bad news has a stronger impact on us than good news—bad news activates our brain's warning system. If we didn't identify, remember, and relay life-threatening information, we would put ourselves and our tribes at risk. That is also why "bad" news travels fast. However, the warning system that once helped us escape from a Sabretooth tiger has now become a detriment to our modern-day well-being. Something as harmless as a backfiring car can trigger our *fight-flight* warning system. This warning system is extremely sensitive and responds to all threats, real and imaginary, in the same fashion. It is at work in every aspect of our lives—there is no "on" or "off" switch. Because this system evolved to detect life-threatening danger, we have a strong response as our muscles tighten, our breath shortens, and our adrenal glands pump stress hormones through our body to get us ready for emergency action.[5] Unfortunately, although our *fight-flight response* is triggered frequently, few situations we encounter in modern society truly require a *fight-flight response.*

Our Fight or Flight System Skews to the Negative

The *fight-flight* warning system resides in the part of the brain called the amygdala. Vigilantly on the lookout for danger, the amygdala uses two-thirds of its neurons to detect negative experiences and then immediately stores them in long-term memory. Positive experiences, on the other hand, get less focus and take at least 12 seconds to transfer from short-term to long-term memory.[6] This warning system is great when you are in the jungle, but is not so helpful when you are in the board room or in traffic. On overdrive, our *fight-flight* warning system causes us to observe and overreact to the bad and play down the good. Do you notice that interesting insights, great conversations and sunsets are often quickly forgotten, whereas intense, grief-stricken traumas are remembered for a long time? Unfortunately, this attachment to bad moments also

5   McLeod, S. A. (2010). What is the stress response. Retrieved from www.simplypsychology.org/stress-biology.html

6   Hanson, R. (2009). *Buddha's Brain: The Practical Neuroscience of Happiness, Love, and Wisdom.* Oakland, CA: New Harbinger Publications.

reinforces our *negativity bias*. Psychologist Rick Hanson explains it this way: "The brain is like Velcro for negative experiences, but Teflon for positive experiences."[7]

We See What We Believe

The negative mindset we're wired for is strengthened by what psychologists call *confirmation bias*, where we filter our reality to confirm our preconceived ideas.[8] We ignore evidence that refutes what we believe and accept evidence that confirms our belief. Thus, if we take a pessimistic view and believe the world is dangerous, our brain filters reality in a way that we prove ourselves right. However, by the same token, if we take an optimistic point of view and believe the world is safe and abundant with opportunity, our filtering mechanism will show us that reality. Our ability to see what we believe is what makes the *What's Going Well* mindset so important: It is a mental strategy that counters our natural tendency to see the negative.

> *"What the human being is best at doing is interpreting all new information so that their prior conclusions remain intact."*
> ~ *Warren Buffett*

---

7   Hanson, R. (2013). *Hardwiring Happiness: The New Brain Science of Contentment, Calm and Confidence.* New York, NY: Harmony Books.

8   Owad, T. (2006). Confirmation bias: A ubiquitous phenomenon in many guises. *Review of General Psychology, 2,* 175–220.

Confirmation Bias in Action

Try this experiment: Look around wherever you are right now and find all the green you can. You may see green in plants, books, curtains, clothes; it doesn't matter—just focus on the color green. Now, without looking up from this page, think about what other colors you saw while you were looking for the green. How many were there? They likely faded into the background while you focused solely on finding green. You only see what you are looking for. That is your *confirmation bias* at work!

Our Reality is the Sum of Our Focus

Much of our life experience is shaped by what we choose to pay attention to—and what we choose to ignore. Have you ever wondered why, when you got a new car, you began to see others like it—same make, model, or color? They were there before but they weren't in your awareness until you owned one. It's thanks to the part of your brain called the *reticular activation system* that is primed to get you to almost unconsciously notice similar cars (or other similarities).[9]

This same system is at work when we adopt a *What's Going Well* mindset; we are creating an elevated awareness where the *neurotransmitters* in the brain start firing and the unconscious mind gets activated to find things that are going well.[10] Those of

---

9   Augustine, J. R. (2016). Chapter 9: The Reticular Formation. (2nd ed.), *Human Neuroanatomy* (pp. 141–153). Hoboken, NJ: John Wiley & Sons.

10   Sapolsky, R. (2005). *Biology and Human Behavior: The Neurological Origins of Individuality*. Chantilly, VA: The Teaching Company.

us who adopt a *What's Going Well* mindset look for the "good" and, in doing so, minimize the "bad." The *What's Going Well* mindset does double duty; it brings positive things into focus while making negativity fade into the background. Also, as we'll see later in this book, things are "good" or "bad" in part because we give them that label. Often an event that we think is "bad" right now, might be viewed as "good" from a different vantage point or in a later phase in life.

We See What We Ask to See

What we ask ourselves matters because it dictates what we pay attention to, and what we pay attention to informs our view of the world. Consider this illustration of the power of our attention. In a study at Harvard University, researchers asked people to watch a video where two groups passed a basketball; the participants were asked to pay attention to the number of times one of the groups passed the ball. In part of the video, a person in a full gorilla suit walked through the groups, arms waving. After watching the video most participants knew how many passes were made, but when participants were asked if they saw anything unusual, more than half did not see the person in the gorilla suit!

What we ask ourselves to pay attention to has a strong influence on what we see; things become visible by virtue of our focus. The *What's Going Well* mindset is a primer for your brain to zero in on things going well. Since "positive" and "negative" things compete for our attention, the *What's Going Well* mindset predetermines which one wins the competition. We want to become experts at finding things going well.

Full Circle

The *What's Going Well* mindset starts a loop that changes our inner dialogue to be more positive, which makes our thinking more positive, which gives us more energy and confidence, which impacts our actions and behaviors, which results in a more positive reality and perspective, which generates more positive thinking and behavior, and so the cycle continues. Also, since most people can only have one thought at a time, a shift to a *What's Going Well* mindset crowds out negative thinking and its draining influence. A mind filled with *What's Going Well* replaces the downward spiral of what's going wrong with a circle of positivity.

What's Going Well Changes the Story

Our lives are dominated by negative stories. These negative stories tend to interfere with our emotions and efforts towards our goals. A *What's Going Well* mindset helps us tell more positive, uplifting stories, which enhance our well-being and contentment.

A Software Upgrade for Your Brain

The *What's Going Well* mindset provides a major upgrade to a system that was primarily devised to detect danger. Much like an old computer, our brains can benefit from an upgrade in software. The *What's Going Well* mindset replaces our outdated *negativity bias* with a more useful *positivity bias*. A change in mindset alters our neurochemistry. When we are focused on *What's Going Well*, our system gets flooded with *serotonin and oxytocin*, two feel-good chemicals that put us in a positive state of mind and help us to be more optimistic and productive.[11]

We Can Teach an Old Brain New Tricks

It was long believed that the brain was static, but as time goes by, scientists are finding more and more evidence that our brains are malleable and that they change in response to our environment and lifestyles. This concept is called *neuroplasticity or brain plasticity*, meaning our brains are constantly reforming.[12] Dr. Eric Kandel of Columbia University, Nobel Prize winner, found that our brains have the ability to reorganize the neural pathways throughout our lifetime. This is great news—we aren't entirely at the mercy of our genetics or our past! The *What's Going Well* mindset can gradually rewire our brain to think positively. Like learning any new skill, the more we concentrate and practice *What's Going Well*, the better we become at using it. More importantly, the more we focus on *What's Going Well,* the more we sculpt our brain's neural structure to make synaptic connections that reduce our *negative bias* and grow our *positive bias*. *What's Going Well* is not just a mindset, it's a mind shift.

---

11   Zahn, R., et al. (2009). The neural basis of human social values: evidence from functional MRI. *Cerebral Cortex, 19,* 276–283.

12   Livingston, R. B. (1966). Brain mechanisms in conditioning and learning. *Neurosciences Research Program Bulletin, 4,* 349–354.

Aggregate Marginal Gains Add Up

Well-being happens one *What's Going Well* moment at a time, and consistently asking the question has a cumulative positive impact on your mindset. Acknowledging small moments of *What's Going Well* fills you up much like a bank account, compounding and increasing your positivity reserves. Just like investing in a 401K every month is wise for your financial future, investing in building strong *What's Going Well* neuropathways is equally beneficial, if not more. These positive moments are what create momentum for a more positive life. Savoring these everyday occurrences will add up to a good week, a great month, and ultimately deep happiness and well-being.

Just as an accumulation of small what's going wrongs can wear down your well-being, a collection of small *What's Going Wells* can enhance it. Focus your attention on small things going well in your life; notice the warmth of the sun on your back, or watching children play at a park. Instead of wolfing down your food, slow down, taste it, enjoy the smells. Notice the difference between dining and eating. Dine on your life by savoring the smallest things going well around you. Over time, small efforts focused on *What's Going Well* can make a big difference in your optimism and the well-being of your relationships, your health, and your career.

What's Going Well Helps Us Navigate the Negative

If we open an email at work that suggests layoffs are possible, the threat of a job loss will undoubtedly trigger stress hormones—the same ones that would be triggered if a lion were charging at us.

Losing your job is a bad deal, but as terrifying and negative as it can feel, it isn't an immediate danger to your life the way a lion could be. A person with a *What's Going Well* mindset may experience the same level of anxiety that an email like this would create. But they would move to recovery faster by focusing on *What's Going Well* (such as having a supportive family, some savings, or contacts in the industry). The *What's Going Well* mindset is not about denying the grimness of the situation, it's about putting things in proper perspective so one can take the necessary action to recover quickly.

The workings of the brain are complicated, but these two points are clear: By design, we've evolved to see the negative and what we see is shaped by what we look for. Harnessing this information, the *What's Going Well* mindset shifts our focus from the negative to the positive and, in the process, vastly improves the quality of our lives.

If we regularly stay in a *What's Going Well* mindset we will see the good in ourselves, notice the good in others and have a more positive outlook. On the other hand, if we have a what's going wrong mindset, we focus on self-criticism, worries, and problems, resulting in a generally negative outlook. *What's Going Well* serves as a mental electrician, rewiring our brains to create the positive change we desire.

In this chapter we've gained an understanding about how our brain can be shaped for a negative or positive mindset, and the benefits of the latter. Next, we'll explore our what's going wrong defaults and then dive into ways to cultivate a healthy, more productive *What's Going Well* mindset in our lives.

three

Understanding Our
What's Going Wrong Default

"If you realized how powerful your thoughts are,
you would never think a negative thought."
~ Peace Pilgrim

Many of us operate from the misguided notion that focusing on problems and weaknesses will somehow help solve them. In reality, focusing on what's going wrong at levels beyond what's needed to address an issue causes more things to go wrong. Having one negative thought makes it easier to have another one, then another and so on. It's simple: the more focus and energy we give to what's going wrong, the more things going wrong we will see. It's that classic slippery slope at work in your brain which creates a negative habit pattern. Is that what you really want?

What's going wrong is insidious and sneaky; it doesn't leave fingerprints, but it has victims everywhere. It distorts our ability to notice the good things in life, infecting the human psyche like an invisible plague. What's going wrong is like an obnoxious person who not only takes their seat, but lays down and takes all the other seats around them so there is no place for *What's Going Well* to sit.

In the last chapter we learned how humans are wired for a negativity bias; here we explore the ways we've been trained and encouraged to focus on what's going wrong. Shining a light on this default mindset helps us recognize these negative patterns and make the shift to a healthier, more productive *What's Going Well* mindset.

We've Learned to Focus on What's Going Wrong

At an early age, we're taught to focus on what's going wrong. I remember when teachers graded my tests in school, they would highlight the questions I got "wrong," usually in bright red ink. However, the answers I got correct were left untouched and unacknowledged. Even our well-meaning parents and coaches get in on the act, pointing out the things we "need" to work on. But often it feels like they're ignoring our strengths. Sure, it is helpful to give and receive constructive criticism. Ironically, being a critic can be a full-time occupation, such as movie critics, food critics, literary critics, etc. But when feedback only focuses on the negative, it diminishes us. We become skilled at identifying and focusing on problems and deficits. Over time, the what's going wrong mindset becomes deeply ingrained and we carry it with us throughout our adulthood. What's going wrong shapes how we think of ourselves and who we think we are, and that matters a lot. This mindset is so pervasive that negativity even affects us when we try to sleep; the things that keep us up at night are usually not the things that are going well. It's time to stop highlighting in red what's going wrong and turn our attention to *What's Going Well*. The more we do it, the stronger our *What's Going Well* mindset will be.

> *"Be careful how you are talking to yourself*
> *because you are listening."*
> *~ Lisa M. Hayes*

What's Going Wrong with Me?

When we turn what's going wrong on ourselves, it leads to self-doubt and criticism that causes needless anxiety, and ultimately inhibits our personal growth and well-being. Imagine that an hour before a big client presentation your mind wanders back to your last presentation, which you felt had some weaknesses even though you landed the client. Your what's going wrong mindset focuses on the negative and recalls how you stumbled over part of your presentation. Even though you recovered and finished well, your negative mindset reminds you how embarrassed you were at the time. This self-criticism causes you to feel fear and anxiety which triggers your *fight-flight response*. You do your best to refocus, but once you calm down you notice a very small stain on your shirt. Even though it is small, you wonder if someone will see it. For the next hour, you criticize yourself in this manner. How do you think this will impact your performance?

If worry worked, there would be no problems.

Somehow we get the idea that being critical and worrying will help the situation, but this could not be further from the truth. We get so focused on our shortcomings that we lose sight of our strengths. Even when we are paid a compliment, we often brush it off instead of taking it in and accepting or even embracing it.

Being conditioned to identify and fix our weaknesses has led many of us to demand an unrealistic perfection of ourselves and others. The absurdity of this was apparent recently when an executive said to me, "I am a perfectionist." I responded by asking, "What are you perfect at?" After an awkward silence, we both broke out in laughter. We believe that we must work hard to be perfect and that to get ahead we must never make a mistake. People often say, "I am my own worst critic," as if being critical of yourself is something to be proud of. Since perfection is an impossible reality, perfectionists spend their lives in a futile pursuit. This is a recipe for failure, because the life of a perfectionist is lived out on a treadmill, chasing something unattainable, accompanied by deep dissatisfaction and anxiety.

"When virtues are pointed out first,
flaws seem less insurmountable."
~ Judith Martin

What's Going Wrong with Others?

In addition to being critical of ourselves, we also have a habit of being critical and judgmental of others, expecting perfection from them too. We often look to find what's going wrong with "them"— talking about what we don't like or what is frustrating. When people don't meet our expectations, our default is to let them and everyone else know. It's even worse if we already have negative feelings about the person. In that case, we are likely to only focus on their faults, as our *confirmation bias* looks for evidence to affirm our already negative opinion. We can get so invested in their faults and what's going wrong with them that we lose objectivity. However, when we turn our *What's Going Well* mindset towards them, we typically can find a number of positive attributes. When you think about it, most people have a combination of virtues and faults: We tend to see the virtues of the people we like and see the faults of the people we don't like.

> *"Great minds discuss ideas; average minds discuss events; small minds discuss people."*
> ~ *Eleanor Roosevelt*

Needlessly talking poorly about others behind their backs is the what's going wrong mindset at its worst. The people involved in these conversations are not only hurting someone else, they're also hurting themselves. One way to spare ourselves and others is by shifting the conversation to *What's Going Well*.

"If you concentrate on what you don't have,
you will never, ever have enough."
~ Oprah Winfrey

Keeping Up with the Joneses

We naturally compare ourselves to others. Doing so can be helpful for gaining perspective, but it can also create resentment, envy, or discontent when we think we need to change in order to "keep up with the Joneses." One way to be miserable is to focus on how great the lives of "the Joneses" must be compared to yours. Since we really don't know "the Joneses" or the struggles and challenges they face, attempting to mirror their lives is unhealthy and unrealistic. Besides, once you catch up with the Joneses, they refinance! Many of the proverbial Joneses that I have met are either miserable or have quit trying to keep up because they've come to realize the undisciplined pursuit of "more" leads nowhere worthwhile.

Our tendencies toward comparison and fear of missing out (FOMO) have become more intense with social media. It's easy to forget that the images and stories shared are carefully curated. In this "perfect" online world that is pure fantasy, there are flawless photos of incredible vacations, epic moments, and professional achievements. There are not too many people proudly posting their break-ups, financial challenges, kids' bad report cards, job losses, or work mistakes. In fact, reports suggest that social media comparison can lead to depression because people get caught up in judging themselves against unrealistic profiles of made-up "perfection," which can create a feeling of not being good enough.[13] The social

---

13   Ferrava, E., Yang, Z. (2015). Measuring Emotional Contagion in Social Media. *PLoS One, 10,* (1–14).

pressure to have it all and do it all is at an all-time high. People are trying to cram more activities into their already overwhelmed lives to keep up. Don't be fooled when some people look like they have it all together—even famous people struggle like the rest of us. As you are looking at someone's photos from Cancun or Bali, the person smiling in the photo might be stressing over how they are going to pay for the trip. A focus on *What's Going Well* can help us be more present and grounded.

> *"Do not spoil what you have by desiring what you have not. Remember that what you have now was once among the things you hoped for."*
> ~ Epicurus

The Infectious Negaholic

At one point or another, we've all encountered a negaholic. They are self-appointed Chief Negativity Officers of the world—a position with no known benefits. Negaholics are what's going wrong experts. They are easy to spot—You can find them almost anywhere, whether it's at home or work. It's also important to be aware that, at times, we all have our own inner negaholic.

The negaholic focuses on the hole, not the donut; the rain, not the rainbow; the thorn, not the rose. Negaholics are world-champion complainers. They say things like, "the hot tub is too hot," "I ate too much," "I can't believe there's no Wi-Fi on this flight," or "I'm always in the slow line." Negaholics believe that misery loves company, so they are more than willing to share their negativity because they want to make sure you join in on the "fun." If they can't find negative things in the present, they will dredge up negative things from the past. They will focus on the negative without acknowledging the positive, continuing the downward spiral of negativity. Even in ordinary situations, negaholics find reasons to be mad and sad. For instance, on a rainy day they will say something like, "What a rotten day." Sure it might be raining, but it is not a "rotten day," a little wet but not "rotten." No matter how positive of a person you are, negaholics tend to suck the life right out of you and anyone in their path. The most important thing you can do when you are around a negaholic is close your mind extra tight! Because our brains have a bias for negativity, negaholics can have a viral-like effect and can infect positive people, much like the flu. If someone started sneezing all over you without covering up, what would you do? Try to distance yourself? What would you say? Ironically, it would make sense to say the same thing to both the sneezer and the negaholic, "Would you please cover your mouth!"

"What you appreciate—appreciates."
~ Lynne Twist

Our Thought Factory

Our minds are thought factories, moment by moment, producing thought after thought. Our minds never seem to cease chattering about everything and nothing, commenting on and judging ourselves and others. Psychologists suggest that the average person has over 75,000 thoughts a day. I imagine most of these thoughts are negative. Our inner voice is constantly babbling negativity and focusing on what's going wrong. Our inner negaholic says things

like: "I'm not tall enough." "I don't have enough." "This won't work."
"I am not making any progress." "I can't do it." "This is too hard."
What do you think is the impact of all this negative thinking?

The Impact of a What's Going Wrong Mindset

Whether from internal or external sources, through our brain
design, or our culture, the what's going wrong mindset harms our
well-being in many ways. Compare the what's going wrong mindset
to a *What's Going Well* mindset below.

What's going wrong (lack of gratitude):	What's Going Well:
• Feeds inner negaholic	• Feeds the positive
• Interferes with enjoyment	• Helps focus on the joy in your life
• Supports addiction to bad news	• Encourages us to look for good news
• Entraps us in a negative feedback loop	• Creates a positive feedback loop
• Projects our negativity onto others	• Spreads positivity to others
• Makes our presence unenjoyable	• Makes us fun to be around
• Cultivates criticism of self and others	• Creates a balanced perspective
• Emphasizes our faults and all that we lack	• Opens our world view
• Creates an unrealistic focus on perfection	• Enhances contentment
• Distorts one's view of life	• Increases well-being
• Causes satisfaction and happiness to be unachievable	

What if you read a book that encouraged you to focus on and journal about all the bad things you experience and witness, and advocated that you repeat these negative stories to your loved ones and coworkers? You would undoubtedly think the author was some kind of lunatic, and likely would reject the advice. Yet, we tend to do this every day, all the while wondering why we don't experience contentment and well-being. Of course, sometimes we need to take a moment to get something off of our chest or confide in others about a problem. What I'm talking about here is the habit and everyday focus of life.

Gratitude Deficiency Disorder (GDD)— a Worldwide Epidemic

We receive and give a lot more criticism than appreciation. Are you suffering from GDD? Many people do. What is the impact of the lack of gratitude and appreciation on our health? Our relationships? Our careers? Our finances? Our communities? According to the John Templeton Foundation, 94% of Americans think that people who are grateful are also more fulfilled and lead richer lives. But less than *half* the people surveyed said they express gratitude on a regular basis—UGH! Insane, right? In other words, people believe that being more grateful will help their overall well-being, but they fail to incorporate it in their lives.

We Have a Choice

Thanks to the digital revolution and our 24-hour news cycle creating instant access to the *mad*, the *bad*, and the *sad* around the world, our focus on what's going wrong has escalated to an all-time high.

Negativity is everywhere: online, on our televisions, in our news-papers, at work, and even in our pockets. It has never been easier to find what's going wrong. As a result, most people have come to *accept* negativity as normal. But we still have a choice: We can succumb to the onslaught of what's going wrong and let it dominate our lives, or we can fight back to regain control of our psyche and well-being.

> *"The definition of insanity is doing the same thing over and over again, but expecting different results."*
> *~ Albert Einstein*

We can't make things better until we stop making them worse. Obsessing over what's going wrong is like digging ourselves deeper and deeper into a hole. This violates the first rule of holes: When you find yourself in one, *stop digging!* If we continue to ask what's going wrong, we continue to cultivate a mindset of scarcity and neg-ativity. Down and down we go.

The most persistent challenges we face in life and work stem from our inherent focus on what's going wrong. Focusing on what's going wrong can result in unnecessary anxiety, pessimism, self-doubt, and self-criticism, which can severely handicap our well-being and cause an unhealthy mental state.

Focusing on what's going wrong is just plain wrong! But it doesn't have to be that way. As the old adage goes, "In order to explore new lands, you have to leave the one you're in." You don't need a new technology or lots of money to gain more optimism and well-being. You need a new mindset—a *What's Going Well* mindset.

> *"You must live as you think,*
> *otherwise you will end up thinking as you have lived."*
> *~ Paul Bourget*

four

Making *What's Going Well* a Habit

"We are what we repeatedly do.
Excellence, then, is not an act, but a habit."
~ Aristotle

D o you have a regular practice of focusing on the things that are going well in your life? If you're like many people, the answer is "no." Sure, you focus on positive things during birthdays, vacations, and other special events. But having a consistent *What's Going Well* mindset and practice can help *every* day be special.

We all have what scientists call a *happiness set point*. It is a point which each of us occupies on the continuum of well-being. In "good" moments you will rise above your set point, and in "bad" moments you will go below it. Over time, without a sustained intentional effort, a person will return to their original *happiness setpoint*. For example, lottery winners experience a temporary rise in their *happiness set point*, but within a short time return to their default set point. Oddly, people who are severely injured in an accident have a short-lived dip below their set point, only to return back to their previous set point before the accident. As you may have already discovered, the promises of infomercials and books with quick fixes to happiness are false. Sure, we may experience a momentary boost in happiness like a sugar rush, but we will quickly return to our set point.

The good news is that we can reset and move our set points to the positive with a sustained daily practice of *What's Going Well*. While genes and early environment play an important role in shaping our disposition, the mind continues to adapt and grow, based on the dominating thoughts it is fed. The *What's Going Well* mindset is the food that nourishes our positive attitude and our well-being, and ultimately helps to reset our happiness set point.

For the most part, something is always going well for us. But we don't always notice. It's remarkable how we can have noteworthy things going for us, but hardly notice them. Sure, we have challenges, but we must be able to turn the *What's Going Well* lens on ourselves. Not only will it help us feel better and enhance our well-being, but it will identify our strengths and highlight our values, which in turn helps us pursue our goals with confidence.

Imagine yourself waking up one morning in a *What's Going Well* mindset. You spend time in bed reflecting on all the things big and small that are going well in your life. You think about the people in your life that care about you, and look forward to lunch with a friend. You consider the fact that you have a bed to sleep in, running water, and food to eat. You note that there may be traffic on your commute, but appreciate that you have a means to travel and time to listen to music or an audiobook on the way. You think about how your contributions made a difference on a project. You grab your *What's Going Well* journal and read some of your previous *What's Going Well* notes, and then make a new entry. You continue your day focused on *What's Going Well*.

Let's look at the same day from a what's going wrong mindset. You pick up your smart phone to turn off the alarm and immediately begin reading about all the death and mayhem in the world. You don't feel energized and you contemplate calling in sick. You think about how bad traffic is getting and agonize about a meeting you have in the afternoon. You turn on the radio to hear more death and mayhem. You're stressed about deadlines, bills, the leaky faucet, and you realize you missed an important message. You continue your focus on what's going wrong throughout the day.

Which scenario lays a foundation for a great day? It's obvious, right? Every moment in what's going wrong takes away from *What's Going Well* time.

A *What's Going Well* Mindset Does the Mind Good!

The goal of a *What's Going Well* mindset is to have us think more about our blessings than our burdens.

"If you want to live a life you have never lived, you have to do things you have never done."
~ Jen Sincero

Grow Your Awareness

"Awareness allows us to get outside of
our mind and observe it in action."
~ Dan Brule

Awareness is key to making any change, because it is always difficult to change what is outside of our awareness and understanding.
What's going wrong is invisible; it doesn't walk up to us and say,
"I'm going to be a problem for you both personally and professionally." Unfortunately, the what's going wrong mindset is so "normal"
that we have grown accustomed to living with it. Not being aware
of this habit prevents us from seeing the harm that it causes. What
we are aware of, we can control—what we are not aware of, controls
us. We must be more aware of where our attention goes.

"It is during our darkest moments
that we must focus to see the light."
~ Aristotle

 journal exercise

Awareness of Negative Thoughts

For an entire day, make note of the negative thoughts and observa-
tions you have by writing them down. Do you notice yourself and
others focusing on *What's Going Well* or what's going wrong? What
internal chatter is dominating your mind? You will be surprised

how much negativity is going on in your mind and around you throughout the day.

Subscribe to the *What's Going Well* journey emails
at gregbellspeaks.com/wgw

Practice What You Know

It's important to note that understanding the *What's Going Well* mindset and living it are not the same thing. Knowledge does not change behavior; *What's Going Well* must be practiced. We all want a quick fix for the challenges in our lives, but that rarely works. When I first started my *What's Going Well* journey, I remember how tough it was. Although I found many things going well, it was challenging to stay in the mindset for long periods of time, because I had the habit of focusing on what's going wrong and I didn't have a game plan or strategy to sustain the positive momentum.

> **A certain amount of unlearning is required to fully embrace the *What's Going Well* mindset.**

Keep the *What's Going Well* Momentum

The habit of a *What's Going Well* mindset is created through the choices we make from moment to moment. These *What's Going Well* moments generate momentum. Momentum is created by taking steady, continuous action. This makes us feel like we are making progress, which builds our confidence. Notice the root word in momentum is "moment," which reminds us to stay in the present; it also has the suffix "um" which reminds us to pause. Focusing on *What's Going Well* causes us to pause to see what is good in the moment. Instead of rushing to the next moment, pause so that every moment can be a *What's Going Well* moment.

Creating a new habit is a fascinating process if you employ your curiosity. Be open to observation and experimentation. Take notice of habits and defaults. Initially, developing a *What's Going Well* mindset may require a good deal of effort. Remember, not only are you battling your own habit of asking what's going wrong, you're also combatting the negative habits of those around you. It may feel a bit awkward at first, but with practice it will become second nature (like the what's going wrong mindset has been).

Create a Game Plan

> *"There is only one way to fail,*
> *and that is by giving up before you succeed."*
> *~ Oliver Lockert*

Making the shift to a *What's Going Well* mindset requires you to be conscious of what you pay attention to instead of living by default, so you'll need to spend some time designing a personalized game plan for doing so. This book and the *What's Going Well? 90-Day Companion Journal* contain a number of battle-tested tools, ideas, and strategies to help you with your journey, but it's ultimately up to you. Don't be discouraged if you feel the *What's Going Well* mindset is not sticking right away. It takes time and commitment before the magic of *What's Going Well* works—be patient and persistent. Also, like any game plan, you may find that you need to make some modifications along the way. Stay focused on the end goal (contentment and well-being) and create the strategy that works for you. Over time, you will get the hang of it and be able to access your *What's Going Well* mindset effortlessly.

What's Going Well Visualization

> *"I never missed a putt in my mind."*
> ~ Jack Nicklaus, Hall of Fame professional golfer

Visualization has been used by athletes, business leaders, and entrepreneurs for a very long time as a way to enhance performance. You can use *What's Going Well* visualization to focus before an interview, a presentation, a meeting, a gathering, or anytime you are feeling anxious about something. Here are the steps:

- Relax and close your eyes
- Take a few slow breaths
- Visualize the situation going well
- Think about things going well in your life
- Feel the gratitude and confidence build within you

The 90-Day *What's Going Well* Journal Challenge

> *"What you do every day matters*
> *more than what you do once in a while."*
> ~ Gretchen Rubin

Thinking about *What's Going Well* is effective, but actively looking for and writing down *What's Going Well* has a stronger and more lasting effect than merely thinking about the good things. In my experience, journaling about *What's Going Well* is powerful and transformative, because on a daily basis I find myself looking for things going well, knowing that I have a commitment to write about them later. For the next 90 days, I challenge you to commit to writing down in your *What's Going Well* journal at least one thing going well in the morning and, right before bed, write down one thing that went well that day. Reflecting on *What's Going Well* in the morning will help you focus on the good before the day's hectic activities and interactions begin to compete for your attention. Find a quiet place at home, or in a coffee shop, a library, or a park. Commit to journaling at the end of the day as well. Right before you go to bed write down at least one thing that went well that day. Observing what went well at the end of the day puts the mind to rest in the positive and can help you get a good night's sleep. These small efforts will create great benefit for your well-being and lead you to a deeper, more profound *What's Going Well* mindset.

Studies vary on how long it takes to create a habit, but it's generally somewhere between 21 and 90 days. Since most of us have been living and working in a what's going wrong mindset for a long time, it can take at least 90 days to make *What's Going Well* journaling a habit.

You don't have to understand science or read long academic journals to know that *appreciation and gratitude can be transformative*. The *What's Going Well* journaling process is designed to let the things going well in your life grow deep inside your mind and help build positive neural pathways that last a long time. Researchers have discovered that the simple act of keeping a gratitude journal can significantly increase your sense of well-being, drive more engagement at work, lower symptoms of physical pain, and lead to better sleep.[14]

Two pioneers in the field of gratitude research, Robert Emmons and Michael McCullough, studied the impacts of journaling—their results were astounding. Participants were divided into several groups and were assigned a daily journaling activity for 10 weeks. The first group spent the time writing about daily problems and hassles. The second group wrote about events that affected them. The third group spent the time writing about the things they were grateful for. Not only did the third group experience a significant rise in their overall well-being, but they had a more positive attitude, exercised more, got better sleep, and reported fewer physical symptoms.[15]

Putting your positive thoughts down on paper is especially important because it helps those thoughts sink into your long-term memory. The act of writing makes the things going well feel more tangible and raises their level of significance, instead of simply letting them unconsciously drift through your mind. It can also be helpful for creating more awareness and supporting your goals. For example, people often aren't too conscious about what they eat on a daily basis, but find that their level of awareness increases and behavior changes when they record what they eat and drink in a

---

14   Wood, A. M., Joseph, S., Lloyd, J., & Atkins, S. (2009). Gratitude influences sleep through the mechanism of pre-sleep cognitions. *Journal of Psychosomatic Research, 66*, 43–48.

15   Emmons, R., et al. (2003) Counting blessings versus burdens: An Experimental investigation of gratitude and subjective well-being in daily life. *American Psychological Association—Journal of Personality and Social Psychology 84*, 377–389.

journal.[16] Similarly, *What's Going Well* journaling fosters a habit of becoming more conscious and self-reflective about everything going well in your life. Reflecting and physically writing down your daily *What's Going Wells* in your journal will help the good in your life stick in your mind and help deepen your habit of finding things going well.

Enhance Your Journaling Practice

If *What's Going Well* doesn't come immediately to mind when you begin to journal, consider the five elements that Gallup measures for determining a person's well-being[17], plus one that I've added:

- Career
- Social (or relationships, both personal and professional)
- Financial (or money)
- Physical (including health)
- Community
- Hobbies (my addition)

It's also helpful to think about *why* something went well. *What's Going Well* or *what went well* is often connected to a particular person, so the exercise can inform you about who you should be expressing appreciation to.

---

16   Kaiser Permanente's Center for Health Research. (2008, July 8). Kaiser Permanente Study Finds Keeping a Food Diary Doubles Diet Weight Loss. Retrieved from https://share.kaiserpermanente.org/article/keeping-a-food-diary-doubles-diet-weight-loss-kaiser-permanente-study-finds/

17   Rath, T. (2010). *Wellbeing: The Five Essential Elements*. Washington, DC: Gallup Press.

As you think about *What's Going Well,* consider your strengths. Initially focusing on *What's Going Well* in terms of your strengths may feel a bit foreign, so one strategy that may be helpful is to think about things that your family, friends and coworkers compliment you on or like about you. For instance, do you have a good sense of humor, are you skilled in relationships, technology, or common sense, or are you someone who can fix almost *anything*? Write specific things in your *What's Going Well* journal with a focus on your strengths and your good qualities. Pay attention to the absence of problems too; maybe your knee doesn't hurt anymore, you have a place to call home, you didn't lose power during the storm, you arrived safely from your travels.

Dividends Are in the Details

"Concentrate all of your thoughts upon the work at hand.
The sun's rays do not burn until brought into a focus."
~ Alexander Graham Bell

Take the time to reflect on specific things, people, and situations that are going well. To get the full benefits of *What's Going Well* journaling, make your entries as specific as possible. Writing, "My work is going well" in your journal is a bit too vague. A more helpful journal entry might be something like, "Project X is ahead of schedule and Jane's part of the project was completed on time and was very well done."

Review your *What's Going Well* journal notes weekly. These positive moments represent your life. They will be informative and inspiring to you in months, or even years, to come. Stick with your *What's Going Well* journaling for at least 90 days—it will get easier as you build momentum. Do your best not to break the 90-day chain, but if you miss an entry, don't stress about it—just start again.

Trade Media Time for *What's Going Well* Mindset Time Instead

When I mention taking time to journal, people often retort, "I don't have enough time to journal." My counter response is, "Are you too busy to be happy? You do have time—You are just choosing to use your time differently." There is not enough time to do every-thing, but you should make the time to do what is important to your well-being. Rather than starting your day by checking in on all the death and mayhem in the world, ditch your smartphone, TV, or radio, and spend time reflecting on *What's Going Well* in your life. Generally speaking, the way you start something is the way it will wind up. Starting your morning with a *What's Going Well* reflec-tion and journaling instead of taking in the news can get your day off to a positive start. Of course, it's important to stay informed, just don't start your day with negativity.

Go on a Media Diet

> *"My desire to be well-informed is at odds*
> *with my desire to remain sane."*
> *~ Anonymous*

Developing and sustaining a *What's Going Well* mindset will be challenging enough in itself; doing so while you continue to consume lots of negative media will make the challenge even tougher. Our well-being is at a disadvantage because on one hand we are being bombarded with negative news and on the other, we look on social media and it appears that our friends and acquaintances are having a better life than we are.

"Where is the knowledge we have lost in information."
~ T.S. Elliot

To increase your happiness and well-being you should ruthlessly reduce your media consumption. For the next 90 days, I encourage you to go on a media diet. Instead of watching, listening to, and reading all the news that you normally do, concentrate on *What's Going Well* in your life. I can already hear the pushback from this suggestion, "I have to stay informed." Informed, yes, but not inundated. When it comes to media, we make the mistake of thinking that more news brings more insight. We must learn to give up some of the news so that we are not disproportionately focused on the bad, to our detriment.

Many of us incessantly check our phones for updates. A study conducted by Asurion, a global tech protection company, found that the average person checks their smartphone once every 12 minutes—up to 80 times a day. Often the good things in our lives are muted by these interruptions. If you find yourself in a negative state or feeling anxious, you should consider limiting your news and social media exposure (or eliminate it all together). It's similar to when people look to change their eating habits. Eliminating or reducing sugar is a good first step towards better health. Likewise, eliminating or reducing media exposure can help you avoid unnecessary negativity and gain more traction towards a lasting *What's Going Well* mindset.

Use devices—but don't be used by them.

Besides the negativity, a real problem with the media is that it moves us away from what's happening right where we are. If N.E.W.S. stands for North, East, West, and South, it points us everywhere but where we are. Just because it's in the news doesn't mean you should pay attention to it. It's ironic that so many of us complain about the media's assault, yet the devices we use to access the media are directly in our control. Turn them off and focus on your *What's Going Well* mindset instead. I know it's easier said than done, but developing a *What's Going Well* mindset and enhancing your well-being is worth the effort.

Immerse Yourself in the *What's Going Well* Mindset

You can dabble in a *What's Going Well* mindset, or you can immerse yourself entirely. Much like learning a foreign language, total immersion works best for training your brain quickly and thoroughly. Intention to lead a more positive life does not occur because time passes—you have to want it, and take action to make it happen.

Make *What's Going Well* Your Greeting

Your normal greeting to your friends and co-workers is probably "How's it going?" or "How are you?" The typical response is either "fine" or an explanation of some problem or issue that's happening in his or her life. None of these responses are helpful or inspiring, and they may even perpetuate negativity. What if, instead, you greeted people by asking, *"What's Going Well?"* Not only will you hear more uplifting conversations, you will also help people reflect on things that are going well in their lives. This will help them develop more appreciation for the things they value and already have, and it will give you a better understanding of the person and what they care about. Besides, it's a much more positive way to greet someone.

You're likely to be met with some confusion or resistance when you greet people with *What's Going Well*, because they're not accustomed to being asked—or even thinking about—*What's Going Well*. When you encounter resistance, be patient. *What's Going Well* can't be imposed on people, it must be discovered. If the person resists or talks about what's going wrong, persist a bit yourself, and ask *What's Going Well?* again. In fact, I will often ask people to share at least *one specific thing* that's going well in their lives—personally or professionally.

When you're able to get people to share something specific going well in their lives, you will see a positive shift in the person you asked. What's more, you will also notice a positive shift in your mood, just from hearing *What's Going Well* for them. Although it requires a level of trust and vulnerability, sharing *What's Going Well* with another person creates good feelings for both of you. In part, that's because it creates *mirror neurons,* which cause us to have similar emotions to those we observe in others. *Mirror neurons* allow us to be vicariously enriched by the things going well for others. For instance, I have made it a habit to ask the baristas at my local coffee shop *What's Going Well?* and it is rare that I am not uplifted by what they share—I imagine they're uplifted too.

An effective *What's Going Well* routine will be personal, so play around to find the best strategy for you. *What's Going Well* might feel awkward and unnatural at first. You'll know it's working when you start to notice more things going well. Learn to see each *What's Going Well* moment as a victory, and savor those victories each and every time. As the saying goes, "A single step does not guarantee a long journey, but you cannot embark on any journey without taking the first step."

Sharing *What's Going Well*

Like flight attendants remind us, put your own *What's Going Well* mindset on first before assisting others. Of course, you'll want to share the *What's Going Well* mindset with others. You'll do so with your greeting and through the positivity that comes with your shift to a *What's Going Well* mindset. You may even find a *What's Going Well* buddy so you can support each other on the journey. Just use caution as you share *What's Going Well:* You don't want to get distracted from your own *What's Going Well* work. You want to be sure you've embraced *What's Going Well* for yourself before encouraging others to do so. This is about your own journey first and foremost. Once that's set, you can think about helping others, but it starts with you.

five

Applying *What's Going Well* Personally

> *"To know others is knowledge.*
> *To know oneself is wisdom."*
> ~ Lao Tzu

In the last chapter we were introduced to the five elements that Gallup measures for determining a person's well-being: career, social (relationships), financial (money), physical (health), and community.[18] In this chapter, we'll consider the last four areas which together give a picture of *What's Going Well* personally. Then we'll explore *What's Going Well* professionally in the next chapter.

What's Going Well with Your Relationships

It's important to focus on *What's Going Well* with our relationships because our well-being is deeply connected to finding the good

---

18   Rath, T. (2010). *Wellbeing: The Five Essential Elements.* Washington, DC: Gallup Press.

within our close personal connections. While a *What's Going Well* mindset is largely an individual effort, it can also be the glue that bonds our relationships. During your *What's Going Well* reflections, both in the morning and at night, think about your most important relationships. Write down specific things you appreciate about an important person in your life in your *What's Going Well* journal. Then, express those thoughts to the person directly. This seemingly small act can pay huge dividends in deepening your relationship.

This focus on *What's Going Well* with relationships can be extended to all close relationships. By concentrating on *What's Going Well* with key relationships, our brain is primed to create stronger, deeper connections. Rarely, if ever, do we hear people talk about what's going wrong in the early stages of courtship, or at the reading of their wedding vows. The *What's Going Well* mindset helps maintain positive feelings and emotions beyond the "honeymoon."

> *"Appreciation is a wonderful thing. It makes*
> *what is excellent in others belong to us as well."*
> *~ Voltaire*

Relationship challenges often are the result of focusing on what's going wrong with the other person. We tend to hold our personal relationships to the unreasonable standard of some imagined perfection, even thinking the other person needs to try harder, be better, and do more. And whenever things don't go as planned, we often blame the other person for what's going wrong. At the same time, we often think they're not being appreciative enough of us! Yet, all the while, we fail to take time to focus on *What's Going Well* with them or in the relationship.

When we are focused on what's going wrong in our relationships, we're unable to recognize the things that are going well. The worst part of focusing on what's going wrong with close relationships is that it's a vicious cycle. We will see more of what's going wrong with them, they will see more of what's going wrong with us, and this will undoubtedly fracture any relationship. It's difficult to communicate with someone—let alone trust them—when we only see what's wrong with them.

The *What's Going Well* mindset helps break the negative cycle by getting us to see the other person's virtues rather than only their faults. We may not be able to influence how someone behaves, but we do have the ability to influence how we perceive their behavior through a *What's Going Well* mindset. Further, when we view the people we are in relationships with through *What's Going Well* glasses, they're more likely to live up to the *What's Going Well* vision of themselves. When we acknowledge and appreciate another's virtues, they are more likely to appreciate ours in return. As discussed earlier, this is explained in part by something called *mirror neurons*: When we observe an action by someone else, a set of neurons lights up in the brain and causes us to have emotions similar to the other person. In other words, when we see the *What's Going Well* in others they will see the *What's Going Well* in us.

 journal exercise

What's Going Well with Your Relationships

Spend three minutes a day for 30 days, actively reflecting and writing all the things going well with respect to a close relationship in your *What's Going Well* journal. Write about the other person's strengths, big and small, and write the things you cherish about that person. Your thoughts and notes don't have to be earth-shattering. This exercise works even better if both parties participate.

Subscribe to the *What's Going Well* journey emails
at gregbellspeaks.com/wgw

"Feeling grateful or appreciative of someone in your life actually attracts more of the things that you appreciate and value into your life."
~ Christina Northrup

What's Going Well Mindset Helps Rekindle Relationships

Perhaps the jokes aren't as funny as they once were, the cute quirk has turned into an annoyance, the novelty of a new relationship has worn off, or there's been a falling out among family members. Somehow we begin to focus on what's going wrong—a surefire way to sabotage a relationship. A *What's Going Well* mindset is the antidote to this relationship pitfall. According to relationship specialist Dr. John Gottman, to maintain a strong relationship, we need five positive moments to counterbalance every negative one.[19] Without a consistent flow of *What's Going Well* in a relationship, the bond starts to erode. It takes determination and hard work to maintain

19   Gottman, J. (1995). *Why Marriages Succeed or Fail: And How You Can Make Yours Last.* New York: Simon and Schuster.

quality relationships, and a *What's Going Well* mindset is a helpful tool to keep our relationships strong.

> **The first step in healing a rocky spot in a relationship is to focus on *What's Going Well* within the relationship.**

Although it is difficult to appreciate someone who doesn't seem to be appreciating you, I encourage you to be the first to take steps towards *What's Going Well*. No matter how challenging things are in the relationship, a *What's Going Well* mindset can help you find at least one thread going well, and you can build from there. The *What's Going Well* mindset gets you to focus on finding the common ground you have with the other person and gets you to think about all that is good in your relationship. Conversely, focusing on what's going wrong tends to pull the relationship apart. We can be the worst critics of the ones we are closest to because we know them so well that we easily see their faults and weaknesses, and we are more inclined to point fingers when we're in conflict. A *What's Going Well* mindset allows those fingers to be pointed at the positives in the relationship. A *What's Going Well* mindset requires us to let go of being an expert at identifying the other person's faults and instead become an expert at identifying their strengths. Sadly, I've witnessed people being overly critical of the people they live with but extremely appreciative of random strangers they may never see again. *What's Going Well* gets us to take in the total picture instead of just the problems. While relationships benefit from other tools and strategies too, adopting a *What's*

Going Well mindset is something that you can do right now and find benefit.

What's Going Well with Kids

It's natural for adults to want to jump in and give ideas and thoughts to children about how they can do better and be better. As a result, we do to children what we do to ourselves: We focus on what's going wrong or what needs to be fixed. All too often, we are obsessed with what's going wrong with children and spend considerable time and energy trying to make them "perfect." This gets passed on unconsciously to the child. Some adults even unfairly compare one child to others, saying things like "Why aren't you more like your sister!?!" Without a doubt, children get a bit weary of the constant criticism without much sincere specific positive feedback. After all, the only things children really want are approval and to know they are loved (probably a little cash too!). Appreciating a child can get a bit complicated if you are constantly reminding them to do this or that. But what if you held your tongue instead of barking advice like: *"clean-up; don't talk with food in your mouth; turn that music down; floss your teeth; do your homework?"* What if you focus on *What's Going Well* and catch them doing things right? This would have a positive impact on their lives and your relationship.

When adults are constantly pointing out fixes and faults, a child is likely to experience low self-confidence and may feel inadequate. When children are taught to obsess over what's going wrong and focus on being "perfect" or getting it "right" they may feel defeated and give up, or grow into adults who have a fear of failure and have a hard time being satisfied with anything short of perfection (the ultimate illusion.) I am not talking about coddling children, nor do I think they all should get trophies merely for showing up. This can cause other problems. But, when children are honestly and consistently praised for their strengths and effort, they are likely to grow up more appreciative and grateful, and to develop an inherent sense of confidence and self-worth. Beyond that, when you share the *What's Going Well* mindset with young people, you are providing them with an invaluable tool for leading a richer, more satisfying life.

Express *What's Going Well*

> *"Appreciation can make a day, even change a life.*
> *Your willingness to put it into words is all that is necessary."*
> *~ Margaret Cousins*

One of the best indicators of a positive, healthy relationship is time spent appreciating each other and expressing gratitude. When you identify specific things that are going well with respect to the relationship, take it a step further and express your gratitude to the person *directly*—everyone wants to be appreciated! There is no need to use fake flattery. Instead, focus on *What's Going Well* to highlight the positive aspects of the relationship.

For example, you could acknowledge your partner for listening to you: "I appreciate you taking the time to listen to my concerns. It means a lot that you are willing to hear me out." A sincere expression of appreciation makes a person feel good, and that effect could last weeks, months, *or even a lifetime*. It may also encourage them to continue the behavior that you're expressing appreciation for.

You will be amazed by how showing gratitude helps your relationships grow. Plus, voicing *What's Going Well* directly to the person allows for a "double dip." According to positive psychology research, the person to whom gratitude is *expressed* feels wonderful, as does the person expressing gratitude.[20] It's a win-win! In addition to deepening and enriching your relationship, expressing *What's Going Well* boosts both parties' well-being much more significantly than if you kept the things going well to yourself.

> "When we express our gratitude to others,
> we strengthen our relationship with them."
> ~ Dr. Martin Seligman, founder of Positive Psychology

What's Going Well Supports Financial Goals

Money is the number one stressor for many people. A *What's Going Well* mindset can provide much needed relief from financial pressures and remind us that money can't buy happiness. What do you notice when you ask yourself *What's Going Well* with respect to money? Maybe you're making progress on payments towards a loan. Maybe you kept your eye out for a sale and scored a great deal on something you've needed. Maybe you reviewed your investments to make sure they align with your values. Maybe you took a look at your budget and found a way to eliminate or reduce items in order to shift funds toward more important goals. The simple act of asking *What's Going Well* with our money can help us get in touch with our values and priorities and take steps to achieve our financial goals.

When we're clear about what we want, the negative feelings associated with cutting back become positive feelings associated

---

20   Grant, A., et al. (2010). A Little Thanks Goes a Long Way: Explaining Why Gratitude Expressions Motivate Prosocial Behavior. *Journal of Personality & Social Psychology Vol. 98*, No 6, (pp. 946–55).

with living our intentions. There will always be someone who has more money, a fancier car, a bigger house, or more glamorous travel. A *What's Going Well* mindset applied to your money shifts the attention from unproductive comparisons with others to productive attention on your own goals and values.

What's Going Well Promotes Health

> *"The first wealth is health."*
> ~ Ralph Waldo Emerson

So often, we take our health for granted until we have an illness. A *What's Going Well* mindset helps us appreciate our health and take care of it. It helps us direct attention to our *wellness* and stay focused on our health goals.

What's Going Well with regard to your health? Perhaps you've committed to a healthier diet, tried a new activity, or met a friend for a walk even though you were tired or the weather wasn't great. A *What's Going Well* mindset helps us remember what *is* working, which can boost our sense of gratitude and our sense of power to take charge of our health. And what about when our health isn't going well? All the more reason to apply a *What's Going Well* mindset right away. We may not get rid of our aches, pains, or illnesses, but we can experience gratitude for what we are able to do and enjoy.

What's Going Well Builds Community

Humans are social creatures with a need to feel connected and valued. We find these connections in both communities of place (such as our neighborhood) and communities of interest (such as a club, group, or league). As with personal or work relationships, we may find ourselves focused on what's going wrong in our community. Maybe you noticed some trash in the park or wish you didn't feel obligated to attend an upcoming community event. Refocusing our attention on *What's Going Well* in our community provides an opportunity to notice the abundant assets around us.

What comes to mind when you ask *What's Going Well* in your community? Perhaps there's a park or coffee shop you like to visit, a neighbor that waters your plants when you're away, or a book group or sports team you enjoy. Thinking about that park, who planted and cared for those trees? Someone you've likely never met has given you and your community a tremendous gift! As you consider *What's Going Well* in your community, think about your own contributions and how great it feels when you lend a hand or pay it forward. A *What's Going Well* mindset applied to our community shines a light on our interconnections and cultivates a sense of belonging. It also fosters a sense of connection and contribution that is important to our well-being.

Ideas and Strategies

The following ideas and strategies can help you keep a *What's Going Well* mindset personally:

1. Put a check on complaining.

Most complaints fall into the *true but useless* category. Have you ever noticed that our complaints are usually about something outside of our control? The weather, traffic, another person's behavior—a complete waste of time and energy! We will never be satisfied or happy spending our time and energy complaining or trying to fix situations that are outside of our control.

It's impossible to complain and focus on *What's Going Well* at the same time. The *What's Going Well* mindset encourages us to give up petty complaints. When you get the urge to complain, ask yourself *What's Going Well* with respect to the situation. If there is something that needs to be taken care of, create a strategy and a plan and then take action. By complaining, I mean useless fussing about things we can't control. By all means, deal with practical issues that need to be addressed. For instance, if an employee has not shown up to work, check in with them. Asking people to stick to their prior agreements or asking the restaurant to serve what you ordered is not complaining. Focusing on those negative things at the expense of enjoying the person or the experience is counter-productive, however.

Refrain from Complaining for a Week:
For a full 7 days in a row, refrain from speaking about what's going wrong. For every negative word, replace it with three positive words.

2. Start conversations with *What's Going Well*.
Make it a habit to insert *What's Going Well* into your interactions with others. When you have the opportunity, ask this of people and also express *What's Going Well* in your conversations. This approach would undoubtedly interrupt the pattern of negativity that can take over in everyday interactions. Imagine if each person

introduces the *What's Going Well* concept to one person a week—
that will be 52 people a year times the number of people! Try it out.
Let's see how far it can spread.

3. Set a timer.

We schedule so many things in our day, yet often run out of time
for the most basic and important things. Break up your day by
setting an alarm to remind you to take a break for a *What's Going
Well* reflection. Along with your journaling, the power of a *What's
Going Well* pause during the day will contribute to strengthening
your *What's Going Well* mindset.

4. Appreciate and praise others.

Make a conscious effort to notice the ways that others are contrib-
uting, and thank them for the effort. Was the clerk pleasant and
efficient? Did the kids put their toys away? Was a meal prepared for
you? Did a coworker do a good job? Did a teacher navigate a class-
room of rambunctious kids? Did the bus driver slow down so you
could catch your stop? Train your eye to notice *What's Going Well*,
and share the gratitude.

5. Pay it forward.

Every day, we benefit from the unnamed generosity of others.
Notice some of your favorite things and consider how they came to
be. That trail by the river, the children's museum, the free concert
in the park? Now think about the talents or gifts you can share to
make the world a little brighter. What might that look like? Could
you volunteer with a neighborhood cleanup, donate to the school
auction, tutor someone, or deliver a meal when someone is ill or

recently had a baby? The ideas are endless and each contributes to *What's Going Well.*

6. Take five steps.

Take one discrete step for each of the five elements of well-being—career, social (relationships), financial (money), physical (health), and community. Choose something small but doable. For example, you might carve out time to connect with a friend or loved one, take a walk, schedule that screening exam you've been putting off, skip one beverage and put the money in your savings account, help a neighbor, or read a book that might up your game. Small steps will help generate a sense of *What's Going Well* and contribute to your sense of accomplishment, confidence, and well-being.

six

Applying *What's Going Well* Professionally

"To win in the marketplace you must first win in the workplace."
~ Doug Conant

How you feel about your work impacts how you feel about yourself and your family, and has a direct link to your well-being. For many of us, work feels like a burden and gets in the way of the good in life. Too often, the only time someone expresses something going well with work is at the end of the day, when they are leaving. You hear comments like, "Whew, glad that's over!" or "Thank God it's Friday!" This is unfortunate, since most of us spend more waking hours at work than any other place, and living merely for time off makes for a sad existence.

Perhaps this feeling is associated with the lack of appreciation often felt on the job. In a recent study by the John Templeton Foundation, researchers found that work is often the *last* place people experience appreciation. Appreciation and recognition are consistently among the top desires of employees around the world, yet these findings, along with other research, show that appreciation is not a central part of workplace culture. Ironically, we're least likely to experience the *What's Going Well* mindset at work, and it just might be the place we need it the most.

Along with a lack of appreciation by others, our negative sense of work is shaped by our own mindset. Whether you work as a utility worker, nurse, CEO, teacher, or computer programmer, the best way to ensure work satisfaction is to cultivate your own sense of appreciation while you work. It's not enough to have a good job and do a good job. You will increase your job satisfaction by focusing on *What's Going Well* in the job. The main reason people have "bad" days at work is because they focus on the negative things at work. Whenever I ask teams about the last time they talked about *What's Going Well* at work, I usually get blank stares followed by "never" or "rarely." Stopping to focus on *What's Going Well* can significantly shift an individual, a work team, or even an entire organization's culture to be more positive and engaged.

What is Your CON (Cost of Negativity)?

A study published in the *Journal of Personal and Social Psychology* found a link between a negative attitude and economic success. Research concluded the cynical participants earned $3,600 less per year than their more positive counterparts. What's the cost of negativity for you? What's the cost of negativity for your organization? We measure a lot of things at work, including time, money, injuries, turnover, and productivity—but what about the cost of negativity? What if we measured the impact of the email pointing out what's going wrong that goes around the office and gets a team off task, or the conflict (and possible attrition) caused by the lack of appreciation of one coworker to another? The focus on what's going wrong is costly. How has negativity impacted your work and your productivity?

Recognizing a *What's Going Well* Work Culture

After years of working with numerous teams and organizations, I have found that one way to tell whether an organization has an appreciative *What's Going Well* culture (or not) is simply to listen to the language the people in the organization use to describe their work, their clients, and their coworkers. People in unappreciative, what's going wrong cultures have negative and unappreciative language. They say things such as "Department X is difficult to work with," "Our clients are clueless," or "I don't like so and so." When we are constantly on the lookout for problems and things that fall short of perfection, we will undoubtedly find them. Unfortunately, we have created workplace cultures that encourage us to look for what's going wrong instead of *What's Going Well*. Many groups don't focus on things going well, yet doing so can inspire us and give us energy to address the challenges that lie ahead.

Cultivating a *What's Going Well* Work Culture

Lack of gratitude is one of the leading causes of workplace dissatisfaction and the cost is high: a workplace culture without gratitude has high turnover rates, burnout, and low engagement.[21] But who decides what kind of culture an organization has? The cultural landscape of an organization is formed by small and numerous interactions with managers, coworkers, and customers. When we focus on *What's Going Well* within our organization, we are helping build and sustain a *What's Going Well* culture. Every time someone thinks or hears *What's Going Well*, it gets reinforced as part of the culture. In other words, an organization's culture becomes *What's Going Well* one *What's Going Well* interaction at a time.

"Where attention goes, energy flows."
~ James Redfield

Genuine Appreciation Yields Results

As important as yearly client and staff appreciation celebrations are, they can be tainted by skepticism if the appreciation isn't authentic and is only happening once a year. Good leaders and managers do their best to create appreciative environments where workers feel valued year round. They understand that a *What's Going Well* mindset at work can contribute significantly to positive outcomes, both for the individual and the organization. A *What's Going Well* mindset puts an individual in an optimistic frame of mind, and interpersonal bonds and team relationships are strengthened at a deeper and more sincere level. The strong relationships that result lead to increased job satisfaction, engagement, and loyalty.

---

21   Armenta, C. N., Layous, K., Nelson, S. K., Chancellor, J., & Lyubomirsky, S. (2016). Functions of Positive Emotions: Gratitude as a Motivator of Self-Improvement and Positive Change. *Emotion Review 1–8.*

Acts of cooperation, teamwork, and empathy generated by the *What's Going Well* mindset also can directly influence an organization's bottom line. The *What's Going Well* mindset is a competitive advantage for organizations that implement it broadly and systematically. While your competitors are focused on problems and negativity, you and your team are focused on the good in the people you work with, your customers, and the work itself, allowing you to see opportunity and growth. There is increasing evidence that companies that have more gratitude and appreciation outperform their peers.[22]

Attitude is Contagious—Spread a Good One

Your mindset definitely impacts your performance, but studies show that your mindset impacts others, too. The person, family, or team with a *What's Going Well* mindset has an advantage because a positive attitude is contagious, and it helps us be more energized, productive, and efficient. And if your business interacts on a daily basis with customers, a *What's Going Well* mindset is more likely to give them a positive experience, increase their likelihood to return, and encourage them to recommend you to others.

---

22 Harter, J. K., Schmidt, F. L., & Keyes, C. L. M. (2002). Well-being in the workplace and its relationship to business outcomes: A review of the Gallup studies. In C. L. Keyes & J. Haidt (Eds.), *Flourishing: Positive Psychology and the Life Well-Lived* (pp. 205–224). Washington, DC: American Psychological Association.

Mind Your Mindset

Even when we're working in a *What's Going Well* culture, our own mindset can bring you or the group down. Consider this example of how our *What's Going Well* mindset can impact us at work.

Jane is a recently promoted salesperson at her firm, and for the first time she has been assigned one of the company's largest clients. The leadership at Jane's firm has started practicing the What's Going Well mindset. After a few weeks, she gets a call on a Monday morning from Karen, her boss. Karen tells her: "Listen, you know I believe in your skills, that's why I promoted you. I have been raving about your knowledge and skills since you got here. The people you are working with directly at Company X are as impressed with you and your work as I am. But somehow, in the first meeting with the client, you rubbed Sally (the department head of Company X) the wrong way." Jane defensively interrupts, "How could that be? Sally was only in that initial meeting for a few minutes, then she had to take a call." Karen goes on to explain that she's not too worried about it since her work has been so outstanding. Karen is positive that Sally will be blown away when she sees Jane's progress and she would like Jane to present a progress report to Sally and her team this Friday.

Despite the high positive-to-negative ratio, what does Jane focus on all week? Of course, the one negative thing that came from Sally. If Jane spends the majority of her time agonizing over this negative element, what will it do to her psyche and confidence when it comes time to present on Friday? If Jane had remembered to apply a *What's Going Well* approach to this situation, she would focus on the positives of the situation, playing up the good elements and downplaying the negative. For instance, Jane could focus on the fact that her boss appreciates and advocates on her behalf, something many people can only dream about.

What's Going Well with Work Relationships

Your work experience is inextricably connected to other people. That's why it's crucial to look for the good in your manager, your co-workers, and your customer or clients, and acknowledge how they play a role in *What's Going Well* for you at work. Unexpressed appreciation is like wrapping a gift and not giving it. Make it a point to think about the leaders and team members you work with and express appreciation to them in a thoughtful and meaningful way. For example, in the middle of a big sales push, you could write a handwritten thank-you note to acknowledge team members' efforts. Don't wait until the end of the year to express appreciation. Do it now!

What's Going Well in Your Current Job

> *"Expectations are resentments under construction."*
> ~ Anne Lamott

Our expectations at work can be complicated. Many people's lives are centered around work, and not just for the money: We often find social status, friendships, and a sense of belonging at work. In truth, we want our work to do and be everything! We long to find purpose and meaning in the workplace. We desire an inspiring manager, fun co-workers, and a positive work environment. Sometimes, these expectations can be so high that it sets us up for disappointment and dissatisfaction. Adopting a *What's Going Well* mindset helps us manage our expectations in a positive way by remembering to savor the things that are going well with respect to work.

> **Warning: *What's Going Well* is a tool to stay positive, not a weapon to avoid challenges.**

Change Your Mindset, Change Your Job

I find it surprising that people who enjoy their work so little stay for so long, without adjusting their mindset. Instead, they choose to blame everyone and everything for their unhappiness—except for themselves. They vacillate between boredom and stress—rendering themselves unproductive, unpleasant, and unengaging—without any personal reflection or intervention to change to a more positive mindset about their work.

It's important to realize that no work or workplace is perfect, and there will always be frustrating situations and co-workers that are challenging to work with. People with a *What's Going Well* mindset make the most of where they are. They understand that developing and maintaining a *What's Going Well* mindset, no matter the circumstances, will determine their work experience and how they are perceived by others. A bad attitude in a good workplace can make the workplace bad. You can have the best job on earth but if you don't have a *What's Going Well* mindset about it, you won't enjoy it. Since your mindset shapes your experience, a change of mindset literally changes the job.

What's Going Well Gets Noticed

Let's imagine you are a manager and have to make a pro-
motion choice between two employees, Liza and Mina,
who have relatively the same skill level and experience.
Liza has said she feels trapped in her current job and per-
ceives it to be boring and unfulfilling. Most of what you
have heard from Liza are complaints about co-workers,
clients, and the job itself. Even though Mina has the same
position as Liza, she frequently points out specific things
that are going well with clients and co-workers, her feed-
back is spot on, and she contributes to improving the work
culture. You can't remember her coming to you with a
trivial complaint. She seems to take responsibility for her
work and is conscious about her impact on those she works
with. Mina's What's Going Well mindset makes her the
obvious choice for the promotion.

Ideas and Strategies

The following ideas and strategies can help you keep a What's Going
Well mindset at work:

1. Start meetings with *What's Going Well*.

Think about the last meeting you attended. If it was like most workplace meetings, it focused on the issues and what's going wrong.
Meetings like this drain the group's energy and zap morale very
quickly. What if, instead, you started your meetings with a conversation about *What's Going Well*? This approach would likely shift
the mood to one of optimism and positivity, and create energy to
take on the projects at hand.

If you are leading the meeting, you can give a few examples of *What's Going Well* to help others think of their own. I found it can have more impact when we share things going well in our personal lives, and not just work. These moments of personal connection help people work better together and increase work collaboration. Spend time before the meeting thinking about *What's Going Well* with respect to the people and the project. After the meeting, write down at least three things going well or that went well during the meeting. Make it your goal to identify all the "bright spots." Of course, merely focusing on *What's Going Well* will not eliminate all the challenges your team faces, but the focus on *What's Going Well* will give your team inspiration and energy to deal with the challenges.

Change the Question, Change the Meeting
Ask *What's Going Well* at the beginning of all your meetings. Have everyone share at least one specific thing.

2. Celebrate.
Typically, success at work is defined by the completion of a task. As soon as a project is done, we quickly move on to the next project, then the next, and so on. This is often done without taking a *single second* to celebrate or acknowledge efforts and accomplishments. Does this pattern sound familiar? If you work this way, a *What's Going Well* mindset is essential to avoid burnout and boredom. Remember, the rat race is run and won by rats!

The *What's Going Well* mindset provides you with a necessary and important pause to catch your breath. It reminds you to enjoy the journey and to capture the lessons the journey may teach. Make it part of your work routine to stop and reflect on *What's Going Well,* especially after a big effort—whether you get the results you wanted, or not.

3. No whining.

Are you whining about your boss or a co-worker? Challenge this self-defeating mindset and instead focus your energy on *What's Going Well.* The more you focus on positivity, the more positivity you'll see. Rise above the negative thoughts and leave the petty gripes to others. It is difficult to win if all you do is whine!

4. *What's Going Well*—a game of 21.

At times, we all need to stop and pump ourselves up about work. Here's a fun game I like to play: Make a list of 21 things going well at work in your *What's Going Well* journal. Record every good thing, big and small, especially the small things that are often taken for granted. Put things on the list like "My computer works," "I get a paycheck," "There's heat or AC at work," "We have electricity." This simple yet powerful exercise can shift you back to a positive *What's Going Well* mindset quickly. And try not to compare your work situation to those of your friends or family. Remind yourself that they have their own unique challenges. You can find joy and fulfillment in your work without comparing it to others'.

5. Implement *What's Going Well* under pressure.

It's much more difficult to focus on a *What's Going Well* mindset when you're feeling rushed, stressed, or pressured. However, these are the times you need it most. Thinking about *What's Going Well* when you're under pressure can help you gain needed perspective to move forward. We all know that stress and pressure to perform are a normal part of work life. Having a *What's Going Well* conversation can give you and your team the boost you need to be even more efficient and successful in times of stress.

6. Turn your commute into gratitude: What went well?
Use your commute home to reflect on what went well at work. Rather than spending your commute getting stressed over work issues, replay everything that went well throughout the day. Reflect on the good. When you arrive home, you'll feel good about the day and be more appreciative. Research has found that the *ending memory* of any situation is critical to how we remember the experience. Therefore, replaying the *good things* that happened at work has a positive impact on your overall memory of the day. Plus, the person who opens the door when you get home will appreciate the positivity coming in. Reflecting on what went well *at work* during your commute not only generates positive thoughts, it may even help you be more relaxed. For example, you may forgive the driver who cut you off in traffic and change yourself from someone with road rage to a road "sage."

7. Use the *What's Going Well* mindset as a competitive advantage.
You can use your *What's Going Well* mindset as a competitive advantage. While others are consumed with negativity, your focus on the good about your job, your company, and your career will not only enhance your well-being, it will also increase your productivity and efficiency. The *What's Going Well* mindset brings about a belief in your abilities by getting you to focus on your strengths. This is not to say you should ignore the gaps or things you should work on, but by focusing on *What's Going Well*, you

will gain the motivation and confidence to handle the challenges and gaps. Further, while others are mired in problems and negativity, your *What's Going Well* mindset will make you stand out from the crowd.

8. Apply *What's Going Well* to routine tasks.
One of the best skills to develop is your ability to have a positive mindset toward routine tasks. One way to do this is to consider how the task is connected to a greater purpose or to the organization's overall mission. Think about how the task is connected to the bigger picture and the positive impact that it has on others. For instance, a loan officer's administrative work for a home loan may seem tedious and boring, but with a *What's Going Well* mindset, the loan officer could visualize the importance of this tedious work to helping a family realize their dream of owning a home. When we apply our *What's Going Well* mindset, we are able to make the connection between a routine task and the bigger picture, thereby executing our work with more focus, purpose and positivity.

Appreciation Increases Engagement
Studies indicate that most people are not fully engaged in their current job—and that their current job is the last thing they appreciate. The connection is obvious: It's impossible to be deeply engaged with something you don't appreciate or don't feel appreciated while you're there.

9. Find a *What's Going Well* partner at work.

One way to maintain a *What's Going Well* mindset at work is to engage in the process with a co-worker. As the Beatles remind us, the journey is always easier with a little help from our friends. So ask a co-worker to be your *What's Going Well* partner. This will help your *What's Going Well* mindset development in two key ways. First, people take on the nature and habits of those they closely associate with, so a *What's Going Well* partner will positively reinforce your efforts. Second, positive peer pressure helps both parties create new habits and stay on track. Get together for lunch or coffee on a weekly or monthly basis to discuss *What's Going Well* at work.

When co-workers focus on and discuss *What's Going Well*—rather than daily gripes and grievances—engagement, teamwork, and productivity are boosted. Time spent concentrating on *What's Going Well* leads to greater understanding of each other and each other's work. This sharing can help break down departmental silos.

And if you are a manager, share the *What's Going Well* philosophy with your team and adopt the mindset in your day-to-day work. If you start every meeting, employee discussion and evaluation of client work with *What's Going Well*, you will see a different attitude develop within your group.

As we discussed in Chapter Two, having *What's Going Well* conversations with others primes the brain for positivity. It creates new neurological pathways that help generate strong feelings of connectedness and appreciation. The positive focus of the conversation impacts the neurotransmitters and almost instantly begins to rewire everyone's brains for positivity.

10. Take control of your own *What's Going Well* mindset.
According to Gallup, a whopping 65% of employees in the US
say they receive no recognition or praise at work. You could wait
around for something that may never come, or you could generate
it yourself by adopting a *What's Going Well* mindset. Not only is it
ineffective to depend on others for *What's Going Well* at work, but
it puts a lot of pressure on you and them. Stop looking to your boss
or coworkers for praise. Generate your own appreciation and make
What's Going Well a vital part of how you approach your work.
Reflect on what you bring to work. Think about your talents, skills,
and strengths. Perhaps it's your attention to detail, your persever-
ance, your patience, or your ability to handle tough client situations.
Since we often take our unique skills for granted, be sure to think
about your unique skill set and your contributions. Think about
What's Going Well with your colleagues or manager, and be sure
to take the time to acknowledge co-workers that are a part of the
things going well for you.

11. Implement *What's Going Well* in Your Organization.
Download the FREE *What's Going Well for Teams Guide – a
10 Step Guide to Incorporate What's Going Well in your Organization* at gregbellspeaks.com/wgw-leaders-guide

seven

What About When "Nothing" is Going Well?

"When one door closes, another opens;
but we often look so long and so regretfully
upon the closed door that we do not see
the one which has opened for us."
~ Helen Keller

It's easy to have a *What's Going Well* mindset when things are, well, *going well*. But what about when life delivers a heart-crushing blow that would make it seem out of the question to ask *What's Going Well*? A *What's Going Well* mindset during challenging times may go against our nature and is not the easiest course of action when faced with difficulties. But in every situation or circumstance—no matter how dire—something is always going well. Asking *What's Going Well* is never out of the question; it is THE question.

"You never know how strong you are until
being strong is the only choice you have."
~ Bob Marley

Difficulties arise in the lives of everyone. I'm as optimistic as they come, but I also know that there's no utopia or storybook ending where everything works out exactly as planned. I have lived long enough to have experienced my share of setbacks. A *What's Going Well* mindset can help us deal with hard times and help us cope with the challenges to get to the other side.

We can't always change the way things are, but with a *What's Going Well* mindset we can change the way we see things. The *What's Going Well* mindset puts us back in the driver's seat of our lives. I wish I had discovered the *What's Going Well* mindset earlier in life—I know it would have helped me get through some challenging times. No, it would not have erased all my losses, but it would have helped me appreciate life more and helped me through heartache and recovery. Often, when a person is going through a tough time, they spend most of their time focused on what's going wrong or what went wrong and do not see or acknowledge anything going well.

Everyone experiences hardships at some point in their lives: How we respond is critical to our recovery and well-being.

Dealing with Life's Setbacks

As Mike Tyson, professional boxer-turned philosopher, once said, *"Everyone has a plan until they get punched in the face."* Whether it's emotional or physical pain, illness, death, job loss, a breakup, or not reaching a desired goal—life cannot be lived without disappointments and setbacks. Even when we have the best-laid plans, life sometimes throws us a punch. If you are over the age of 13, life has probably delivered some serious punches to the face. Yet, as I've come to learn, one can always find good in the bad. Without dark, we cannot know light. Psychologist Carl Jung explained it like this: "There are as many nights as days, and the one is just as long as the other in the year's course. Even a happy life cannot be without a measure of darkness, and the word 'happy' would lose its meaning if it were not balanced with sadness."

Knowing that punches and setbacks are a part of life, we see that our response to the disappointment is where the real opportunity lies. Staying true to the *What's Going Well* mindset during a rough patch is where it can really show its value. A tough setback demands our full attention; job loss or a distressing diagnosis can be brutal on the psyche. But just because you get bad news does not mean you have to become the bad news. I'm not saying that we should avoid mourning a loss, especially when life drops us to our knees. One must take time to process and grieve. There is a point, however, when dwelling on what's going wrong is detrimental to recovery and well-being. A *What's Going Well* mindset can help us move forward despite the situation.

> *"The last of human freedoms*
> *is to choose one's attitude in*
> *any given set of circumstances."*
> *–Viktor Frankl*

What's Going Well Builds Resilience

Research indicates that people who cultivate a positive attitude of appreciation over time build up their emotional immune system. This internal defense serves as a soft pillow when they fall on hard times. There's also evidence showing that people who focus on *What's Going Well* are more immune to stress. Whether that stress is from insignificant annoyances or major life challenges, those who focus on positivity tend to be more resilient during hardship.[23]

While you can't control everything that happens, everything that happens can benefit from a *What's Going Well* mindset. We all experience events that take the wind out of our sails or send us into a tailspin. During these times, a *What's Going Well* mindset can be just the spark you need to shift perspective and get back on track. Directing your attention towards *What's Going Well*, even for just a few minutes a day, can fuel hope and inspiration and keep you going. A *What's Going Well* mindset will not necessarily make the challenges disappear, but it is the beginning step to healing and recovery.

"Rough seas make better sailors."
~ Unknown

---

23   Emmons, R. A. & McCullough, M. E. (2003). Counting blessings versus burdens: An experimental investigation of gratitude and subjective well-being in daily life. *Journal of Personality and Social Psychology, 84,* 377–389.

Choose Your Response, Change the Impact

People react to setbacks in a number of different ways. Some people "freeze." They feel overwhelmed and become catatonic. They feel helpless and have difficulty coping. Some people emotionally explode. They "fight" and rage against anyone and everything in their path. Some people become victims—they blame others and the world, and say things like "Look at what they did to me," or "This isn't fair." There is another group of people that seem to bounce back relatively quickly and often come back stronger and more resilient than before. They have a *What's Going Well* mindset—they look for *What's Going Well* with respect to the situation and find things going well where others only see problems. They are able to convert a career loss into a better career opportunity. Consider Oprah Winfrey, who was let go as a news reporter and told that she was "unfit for television news." She was devastated, but took advantage of her demotion to take a job with daytime television, which was viewed as a huge step-down at the time. The rest is history. The Oprah Show became one of the most successful shows in television!

"That which does not kill us, makes us stronger."
~ Nietzsche

Imagine that a person spends years writing a book, only to have their car window smashed and their backpack holding the only copy of their handwritten notes and manuscript taken from their car. Asking *What's Going Well* might seem ridiculous at that moment. Or, it could help restore calm and start recovery. Reflecting on

What's Going Well, this person might conclude that things could have turned out much worse: "At least I wasn't physically harmed," "I am glad I have insurance and can replace my window," "I wrote the book once, I can do it again." Thinking and journaling about *What's Going Well* in a situation like this can provide the energy and resiliency to follow through and do what's necessary to move on and complete the book.

Now let's take the same scenario, where a person gets their backpack stolen from their car, but this time they focus on what went wrong. They obsess about how unlucky they are and start recounting other bad situations from their past, thinking to themselves "I will never find the time to recover all of the research and writing;" "This always happens to me, I am so unlucky." They become so distraught about being victimized they do not report the crime or call the insurance to get the car repaired. Any time they get the chance, they talk about how bad it was for them to lose their book, journals, and other items. This goes on for weeks, months, and then years. As a result, the problem is exacerbated as they become so agitated and distraught by the situation they never get going on rewriting their book. They become known as "the person who lost their book."

This scenario is not made up. It happened to me, and the book I am referring to is the one you are reading. Yes, I had my car broken into and all of my work stolen including journals, research notes, and the draft manuscript. It was heartbreaking, because I had put in years of work researching and studying gratitude and appreciation. I imagined the thief just threw the journals and the manuscript in the garbage and kept the backpack and the other valuables contained in it. Soon after my initial shock of seeing my car window smashed and my backpack missing, I did reflect and journal about

What's Going Well. The first thing that popped in my mind was: "Imagine the great story that I will be able to tell about how a book focusing on the importance of *What's Going Well* was stolen from my car." I knew the unfortunate situation would delay the book project, so I didn't whistle and skip back to my office in a joyful *What's Going Well* mood. It took a while to get to that point, but it was the *What's Going Well* mindset that helped me recover and persist with the completion of the book.

"In the depth of winter, I finally learned that within me there lay an invincible summer."
~ Albert Camus

Change is Always Happening

Focusing on *What's Going Well* while you are in a challenging situation is not easy. You have to allow yourself time to grieve and feel the loss, but you must realize this state is temporary. As impossible as it may seem, you will find a way forward. A *What's Going Well* mindset can help you recover, heal, and grow stronger.

A Victim Mentality Creates Victims

Sadly, some people get stuck in the victim mentality, even when the challenge is long past. Some find it is easier to blame others and assume the role of victim without taking responsibility for how they respond. No matter what, they refuse to take steps to recover and continue to blame others, rather than choosing to move forward or take positive actions to better the situation. The victim mentality not only avoids personal responsibility, but it also gives away our power, rendering us helpless and hopeless. If we are focused on what's going wrong in our lives, we are frequently in a lousy mood and often feel like a victim. However, few circumstances are entirely bad or good. From time to time, everybody has challenges, but some people define themselves as the victim, no matter the circumstances. Of course, there are people who have been victimized and have a very difficult time recovering to normalcy in their lives. However, hiding behind the claim of victim and not taking responsibility for our mindset can completely disempower us.

The *What's Going Well* mindset is designed to refuel our optimism and give us hope so we can get back on track. Helplessness and hopelessness lower our productivity and our ability to face challenges. There are many things in life we cannot control, but our mindset is not one of them. The word *responsibility* means the ability to respond. We are responsible for how we respond to situations. In tough situations, our ability to respond might be constrained but ultimately, it is up to us. The *What's Going Well* mindset can put us in the right mental state to respond appropriately without making excuses, blaming others, or waiting to be rescued. A *What's Going Well* mindset will help you take 100% responsibility for what you pay attention to in any given situation.

A disaster can often turn into a blessing in disguise. To find the blessing, one must be willing to look for it. Interestingly, studies show that people who cope well in challenging situations feel a greater responsibility in how their lives go. People who blame their circumstances and others tend not to believe their personal efforts matter, and tend not to cope well in challenging situations.

A *What's Going Well* mindset reframes our perspective; it helps us confront and manage situations rather than just react to them. One of the most ineffective strategies for overcoming a "bad" situation is dwelling on it rather than taking responsibility and focusing on how to effectively move forward.

> *"Every adversity carries with it*
> *a seed of an equivalent greater benefit."*
> *~ Napoleon Hill*

No Presents at a Pity Party

In times of stress, it's common for people to focus on negativity and what's going wrong. But this default attitude and approach often aggravates the problem and makes matters worse. Besides, no one likes pity parties because there are no *"presents"* or presence.

What's Going Well: Reframing a Crisis

> *"Barn's burnt down . . . now I can see the moon."*
> *~ Masahide, Japanese poet*

The *What's Going Well* mindset is not about ignoring all negativity, disregarding life's challenges, or denying that suffering exists.

Rather, it's about not letting the challenges and setbacks dominate our mind, so we can move forward. During a crisis, *What's Going Well* can:

- reframe setbacks into positive outcomes;
- empower you to transform challenges into opportunities;
- allow you to focus on what you can gain or learn from tough situations;
- cultivate meaning and purpose beyond the current situation; and
- create a balanced perspective.

It is more beneficial to focus on lessons learned than to sulk and lament about the negative situation we may find ourselves in. Rather than wallowing in self-pity, a *What's Going Well* mindset makes problem solving possible. Whining and complaining in the moment may seem like a good idea, but deep down, we know it's a waste of time and energy.

When Bad is Good

"Things that were hard to bear are sweet to remember."
~ Seneca

It's common for people to become complacent or feel entitled when things are going well. But here's the reality: Everything we have can be taken away in an instant. Experiencing hardships can help us stop taking things for granted and be more appreciative of what we have. It can also help us learn valuable lessons and grow from the experience. As we reflect on past unpleasant experiences, it's not helpful to dwell on what went wrong. Viewed through a *What's Going Well* mindset, these events can remind us that we have and can overcome challenges. It may even help us feel more thankful for our current situation. For instance, a person who grew up in abject poverty—who now has an education, career, and a place to call home—can find plenty of things going well relative to their past, just as a person who has overcome a health scare is able to appreciate where they are now relative to the challenge.

From the Biggest Pile of Manure
Can Rise the Sweetest-Smelling Flower
The goal of focusing on past situations is not to re-injure yourself, but to gain a positive perspective on your situation today. It makes little sense to rehash past challenges without seeking the lessons or gaining some insights.

A Matter of Perspective

Consider this example of how a *What's Going Well* mindset can work in tough situations. Imagine two employees who do similar work at the same company, who both lose their jobs in a layoff. This loss of employment is not due to performance; rather, it's the result of a change in direction of the company. Person A (whom we'll call "Jerry") takes a *What's Going Well* approach, and Person B (whom we'll call "George") takes a what's going wrong approach.

What's Going Well approach
In response to this situation, Jerry:

- reflects on what went well at the job, the things he learned, the contacts he made.

- thanks his boss and coworkers for the opportunity.

- dusts off his resume.

- appreciates the severance package and free time to spend with his family.

- anticipates a positive next step.

- applies for jobs and expects the best.

- reaches out to people and lets them know he's looking for an opportunity.

What's going wrong approach
In response to this situation, George:

- falls into victimhood.

- says things like "Why did this happen to me?" and "This isn't fair."

- looks for people to blame—his coworkers and his boss.

- tells everyone around him how "bad" things are.

- speaks badly about the company.

- sinks into depression.

Same event, different perspectives. George's what's going wrong mindset derails him from getting back on track, and it hurts him more than necessary. But Jerry, who took a _What's Going Well_ mindset, soon finds himself gainfully employed, with his overall well-being intact. As Jerry focuses on _What's Going Well_ during a difficult time, he experiences less negative impact. In short, he is able to move forward to the next opportunity relatively quickly, with less stress.

 journal exercise

What's Going Well—Negative to Positive

Spend 15–20 minutes recalling a situation that seemed negative at first but turned out to be positive in the end. Make a list of the things that went well with respect to the situation in your *What's Going Well* journal.

Subscribe to the *What's Going Well* journey emails
at gregbellspeaks.com/wgw

When a Tough Time Comes

When faced with hardship, take a *What's Going Well* approach to help you move forward. Use your self-awareness and acknowledge the reality of the situation. Think of *What's Going Well* as a method to enhance your well-being and move you into positive action. Cultivate *What's Going Well* by considering:

- What resources are available to help?
- What can I learn from this?
- How can I benefit from this situation?
- Who else in my life has overcome this?
- How have I overcome challenging situations in the past?

Success and well-being are a matter of finding positives amidst the chaos. Rarely does a person have everything going well in their life. Your ability to succeed is determined by your mindset as well as your circumstances. Relying on your *What's Going Well* mindset during hardships will help you overcome pain and challenges to become a stronger and more resilient version of yourself.

eight

Final Thoughts:
Turning Knowledge into Action

"Have patience with all things,
but first of all, with yourself."
~ Saint Frances de Sales

We humans are absolutely remarkable—true miracles. To be who you are is a statistical miracle. Scientists say the chance of being born is one in four hundred trillion, or another way to think about it—one in infinity. But, we must be in the right mindset to take advantage of this fact. The *What's Going Well* mindset helps us expand our worldview and remain the positive miracles that we are.

Of course, there will always be sad, frustrating, and negative things threatening your positivity. Whether it's rudeness of another person, an unexpected setback, or a global catastrophe—

experiencing negativity is part of being human. But being human also means we hold the power to choose what we focus on. Don't let negativity live in your mind rent-free. Each day on this earth holds something joyful for you—as long as you're willing to find it.

Preparing for the Journey

Throughout this book, we've explored negativity, positivity, and how your mindset impacts your overall well-being. We've discussed how persistent negativity perpetuates dissatisfaction, and how negative thinking is a product of both our human nature and the world around us.

But we've also learned that there's a proactive way to break the negativity cycle for good: The *What's Going Well* mindset. We've learned that *What's Going Well* is not about being happy at all times, but about focusing on the good in our lives to cultivate well-being and resilience. We *understand* that the *What's Going Well* mindset is the antidote to negativity and its damaging effects. We *know* that we hold the power to avoid the damage and poison of negativity by focusing on the good, each and every day. And finally, we *believe* that every day is a celebration; that each moment is something to be thankful for.

Reading this book is a first step towards creating a more positive and fulfilling life. Understanding the concepts outlined in *What's Going Well?* is important and valuable, but understanding won't bring the concepts to life. The change starts when the work begins, with diligence, self-reflection, and effort. Let's recap some of the key themes we've covered.

Recognize and Reject Negativity

Acknowledging the negativity in your life is the first step towards redirecting your focus. When you notice negaholics around you and within your own mind, intervene. Protect yourself from their damaging effects. Refuse to let them dampen your spirit. Without intervention, negativity permeates your positive mindset. It becomes habit. Take a proactive approach to the factors shaping your reality. Remember: The mind is like a garden—we harvest what we sow and care for. Asking what's going wrong, even when trying to solve a problem, is like watering and feeding a bed of weeds. The more you focus on the problem, the bigger it gets.

Embrace the *What's Going Well* Mindset

What's Going Well is an antidote to negativity. Use it to find hope within our problem-focused culture. Use it to see the good that's right in front of you, at this very moment. Train your brain to see what you have *already accomplished* and rejoice in how far you've come. Change your internal language, find the silver lining, and embrace a state of relentless positivity. Zeroing in on *What's Going Well* in all areas of your life will reveal an infinite waterfall of good.

Spread Positivity at Home

A *What's Going Well* mindset at home is vital to your greater well-being. Your home should be a place of peace, rest, and rejuvenation. Unplug and recharge. Take a break from technology and spend time with your family focused on *What's Going Well*. Talk with your partner and close relations about *What's Going Well* every day. It's a great way to cultivate stronger connections and a more positive, harmonious environment.

Be *What's Going Well* at Work

Having a *What's Going Well* mindset and work culture will lead to more engagement and productivity. Practice your *What's Going Well* mindset at work to find for yourself and others the things that are going well within your organization. Spread *What's Going Well* in meetings, on your commute home, at the water cooler, and on your lunch break. Embrace *What's Going Well* for those around you: be open to new ideas, foster relationships, and express gratitude to co-workers, even for small things. Whether or not others join you on the journey, a *What's Going Well* mindset will make you better in your job and happier in your career.

Make *What's Going Well* Your Reality

Like most things worth doing, asking *What's Going Well* is easier said than done. So, make it a daily routine. Practice becomes habit; habit becomes reality. Changing the way you think and interact is the only way to make a positive mindset work. Instead of asking: "How are you?" ask "*What's Going Well?*" Doing so helps spread happiness and well-being. Most people will enjoy it, some won't. It may be uncomfortable at times. Don't take it personally—this is the society we live in. When you find resistance, persist anyway. Do this when you can, but ask *What's Going Well* of yourself first.

Become the positivity you want to see in the world and trust that the rest will follow.

Turn Words into Practice

Have a *What's Going Well* day. Choose an ordinary day, with nothing special or notable planned. Put down your smart phone, turn off the TV, set down that newspaper. Reflect on *What's Going Well* for a full 24 hours. Immerse yourself in positivity. Start your *What's Going Well* journal; commit to writing in it every day for 90 days. Take inventory of all that is good and well in your world; the things that might take time to see. Work on refining your appreciation skill. Be gentle on yourself if it doesn't come easily right away. You're countering deep habits and a culture that defaults to negativity. But if you give it 90 days, I assure you, you'll see a difference.

Infuse Yourself with Positivity

When life is difficult, and times are challenging, you may have the inclination to wallow in self-pity. Resist this temptation. The world is not against you. We can all use the *bad* to show us the value of the *good*. If life were without challenges at all times, we would forget to be appreciative. Don't allow yourself to feel entitled. Seize the opportunity for growth and navigate challenges by asking *What's Going Well*, even while you are in the midst of a difficult or painful situation. Tough times are a part of life. Asking *What's Going Well* can offer some relief and direction. With a *What's Going Well* mindset, the challenging, stressful, or sad times will have great value as you remember what you've endured and feel a sense of pride for what you've overcome and of what you have become.

Stepping into the *What's Going Well* Journey

This book began with a true story about a simple question: *What's Going Well?* That simple question had such a profound effect that it sent me on a journey to understand and share the power of the question. This book contains lessons, practices, and ideas to help you with your *What's Going Well* journey. The effort will be worth it. Remember, you've got nothing to lose but negativity and everything going well to gain.

acknowledgments

There are so many people that have helped me with this book. Without a doubt this book has been shaped by many people in my life.

Thank you to Robin Carter; her ability to listen and provide feedback on the book in the initial stages helped me realize that this was a worthy concept. Although the early conversations were a bit clumsy, her ability to listen and question my thinking helped me articulate the proper framework for this book.

Thank you to Janet Hammer; she is the type of person and friend that everyone should have in their life—talk about *What's Going Well*. She brought a breath of fresh air and valuable insight to this book with the grace of a saint.

Thank you to Kate Carman, a gracious giver who helped me bring this project to a whole new level. She has been so generous with her time and advice. Her generosity went beyond measure! It will take lifetimes to repay her kindness.

Thank you to Patty Farrell; I am forever grateful to her for the wisdom and kindness over the years. She brought intelligent insight and clarity to this book.

Thank you to Dick Slawson who painstakingly read and reread early drafts and yet continued to encourage me.

Thank you to my wonderful sister, Karen Wilson, who has encouraged me since I was young. She talked through ideas and read drafts early on and provided helpful feedback.

To my wife, Claire, who is my *What's Going Well* partner for life. She understood and supported the idea of this book from the beginning. I am lucky to have her on my side.

Thank you to the readers of the manuscript for your time and smarts. Your insight and input have enhanced the quality and content of *What's Going Well?* Your feedback informed me and your encouragement inspired me. I am forever indebted to all of you:

Sydney Bell

Megan O'Kelly

Michele Hasle

Marisa Hodes

Devon Neves

Grace Moen

I have been blessed with a network of friends and family too large to name here, but a special thank you to the following people who have been an integral part of *What's Going Well* in my life: David Rae, Roland Hoskins, Aaron Thomas, Mark Few, Ken Sprague, Landon Crowell, Reva Kopel, Tim Morgan, Daric Ashford, Marc Patrick, Jodi Guffee, Shaleta Dunn, Chad Doing, Shawn Busse, Kevin Carrol, Seth Walker, and Brandon Laws.

I am excited for the new *What's Going Well* relationships this book creates.

about the author

Greg Bell

Greg Bell is an author, motivational speaker, thought leader, and business consultant. He has inspired an array of organizations, from Fortune 500 companies like Nike, Disney, and Comcast, to athletic teams like the Portland Trailblazers, Oregon Ducks Football, and Gonzaga Bulldogs Basketball.

As an innovator and keen observer of highly successful leaders and teams, Greg has learned that the key to success is having the courage to use the skills you already have to achieve a result greater than you previously imagined.

Inspiring and energizing audiences with his engaging storytelling, Greg shares his knowledge with excitement and passion. His ability to masterfully blend insight and encouragement with just the right dose of reality makes him the consistently top-rated keynote speaker at major conferences. A Certified Speaking Professional (the highest earned designation from the National Speakers Association), Greg influences thousands of individuals and teams each year with his innate ability to connect personally with audience members.

Whether you're rolling out a new culture initiative, developing your leaders, or seeking a keynote that will be remembered long after your event, Greg will deliver a tailored session that will encourage and inspire each attendee to become stronger, more empowered, and more productive than ever before.

Greg holds political science and law degrees from the University of Oregon, where he played Division I basketball and was consistently named Most Inspirational Player. He is also the force behind Coaches vs. Cancer—a campaign for the American Cancer Society that has raised over $100 million for cancer research. In addition to his corporate leadership experience, Bell is a TEDx Talk alum, serves on the advisory board for the Portland TEDx conference series, and is a Trustee for the University of Oregon Foundation.

Greg lives in Portland, Oregon with his wife Claire and has three daughters, whose middle names are Grace, Hope and Joy.

Greg Bell Seminars

To learn more about Greg's keynotes and leadership seminars, or to book Greg for your event, visit gregbellspeaks.com/book-greg or call 1-877-833-3552. Greg looks forward to customizing a program for your next event!

Ordering Information

To buy multiple copies of this book or journals for your team, go to gregbellspeaks.com/books.

additional resources

Subscribe to the *What's Going Well* journey emails
The *What's Going Well* journey emails provide you with ongoing reminders to reflect on *What's Going Well* in your life. The emails are a perfect companion to the book and 90-day journal—gregbellspeaks.com/wgw

Download the *What's Going Well for Teams Guide*
This free guide provides a 10-step process for incorporating the *What's Going Well* principles into your organization—gregbellspeaks.com/wgw-leaders-guide

See Greg Bell's Recommended Reading List
For Greg Bell's recommended reading list, go to gregbellspeaks.com/reading-list

stay connected

Sign Up for Greg Bell's Newsletter
Receive helpful reminders and tips. Sign up at gregbellspeaks.com

Attend a Seminar
If you want to be the best at what you do, join Greg at a public seminar. Learn more and register at gregbellspeaks.com

Follow Greg on Social Media

 @gregbellspeaks

 @gregbellspeaks

 @gregbellspeaks

Get More Information and Visit the Website
For extra content, support, guides, or to contact us, visit gregbellspeaks.com

Printed in the USA
CPSIA information can be obtained
at www.ICGtesting.com
CBHW071254290424
7671CB00005B/10